Depression

We live in an era of depression, a condition that causes extensive suffering for individuals and families and saps our collective productivity. Yet there remains considerable confusion about how to understand depression. *Depression: Integrating Science, Culture, and Humanities* looks at the varied and multiple models through which depression is understood. Highlighting how depression is increasingly seen through models of biomedicine—and through biomedical catch-alls such as "broken brains" and "chemical imbalances"—psychiatrist and cultural studies scholar Bradley Lewis shows how depression is also understood through a variety of other contemporary models. Furthermore, Lewis explores the different ways that depression has been categorized, described, and experienced across history and across cultures.

Bradley Lewis is Associate Professor at New York University's Gallatin School of Individualized Study with affiliated appointments in the Department of Psychiatry, the Department of Social and Cultural Analysis, and the Division of Medical Humanities. He has dual training in humanities and psychiatry, and he writes and teaches at the interface of medicine, humanities, cultural studies, and disability studies. Lewis is the author of *Moving Beyond Prozac, DSM, and the New Psychiatry: The Birth of Postpsychiatry* and *Narrative Psychiatry: How Stories Shape Clinical Practice.*

The Routledge Series Integrating Science and Culture
Editor: Lennard Davis, University of Illinois at Chicago

The Routledge Series Integrating Science and Culture aims to reunite the major discourses of science and the humanities that parted ways about 150 years ago. Each book picks an important topic that can best be understood by a synthesis of the best science and the best social and cultural analysis. In an age when more and more major political and life decisions involve complex understandings of science, medicine, and technology, we need to have a bioculturally sophisticated citizenry who can weigh in on these important issues. To that end these books aim to reach a wide swathe of people, presenting the information in readable, illustrated, succinct editions that are designed for classroom and scholarly use as well as for public consumption.

Available
Autism by Stuart Murray

Forthcoming
Culture by Nicole Anderson
Love by Lennard Davis
Sex and Gender by Anne Fausto-Sterling

Depression

Integrating Science, Culture, and Humanities

Bradley Lewis

New York University

Routledge
Taylor & Francis Group

NEW YORK AND LONDON

First published 2012
by Routledge
711 Third Avenue, New York, NY 10017

Simultaneously published in the UK
by Routledge
2 Park Square, Milton Park, Abingdon, Oxon OX14 4RN

Routledge is an imprint of the Taylor & Francis Group, an informa business

© 2012 Taylor & Francis

Library of Congress Cataloging in Publication Data
Lewis, Bradley.
Depression/Bradley Lewis.
  p. cm. — (The Routledge series integrating science and culture)
  1. Depression, Mental. I. Title.
  RC537.L487 2011
  616.85'27—dc23   2011017460

ISBN: 978–0-415–87720–6 (hbk)
ISBN: 978–0-415–87721–3 (pbk)
ISBN: 978–0-203–35732–3 (ebk)

Typeset in Adobe Caslon and Copperplate by
Florence Production Ltd, Stoodleigh, Devon, UK

Printed and bound in the United States of America
on acid-free paper by Walsworth Publishing Company, Marceline, MO

Contents

PART III: THEORETICAL AND CLINICAL CONCERNS

SERIES FOREWORD

The Routledge Series Integrating Science and Culture aims to restore connections between the sciences and the humanities, connections that were severed over 150 years ago. This mutual exclusion was done in the name of expertise on the part of science and defended in the name of preserving values and morality in the world of humanism. In some sense, each side was seen as the societal enemy of the other. From the humanists' perspective, scientists threatened to make the world a colder, more efficient place lacking in feelings and values. From the scientists' viewpoint, humanists were interfering with progress by injecting bleeding hearts and unreasonable fears into an essentially rational process.

But the reality is that now, in the twenty-first century it is getting harder and harder for humanists to comment on civic and social matters without knowing something about science, medicine, and technology. Suddenly there is the need to understand stem cells, brain scans, DNA technologies, organ transplants, ecological outcomes, and the like in order to be a knowledgeable citizen, legislator, or scholar. Likewise, scientists routinely include the ethical, social, cultural, and legal in their research protocols and scientific articles. The divide between the "two cultures" described by C. S. Lewis in the 1950s is less and less possible in the twenty-first century. On the ground, humanists and scientists are again in need of each other.

To that end, the books in this series will focus on the cultural side of science and the scientific side of culture. David Morris and I have coined the term "biocultural" to indicate this new realm of study and critique. In that spirit, Bradley Lewis's book on depression aims to bring together in a truly interdisciplinary sense the best of both knowledges on this pressing social and scientific subject. Lewis's book will be the first not only to bring together the latest knowledge on neurology, psycho-pharmacology, genetics and the like, but also to include the cultural (medical and popular), social, political, and historical elements as well. Lewis's major question is—can we know depression only by clinical and research means? To what extent does the patient's experience work into any explanation of a complex phenomenon such as depression? The culture presents us with so many ways of understanding, knowing, and interpreting the symptoms that have come to coalesce around depression. Can we ever see depression as a purely diagnostic term without pulling in the complex knowledges involved in a biocultural analysis? Lewis is also very interested in narrative psychiatry, and so his analysis reflects the ways in which language, storytelling, and life-stories play into any significant understanding of depression.

Lennard Davis
Series Editor

PREFACE

Depression is a topic that touches almost everyone. The numbers are so prevalent that most people will either be diagnosed with depression or will have a close friend or family member diagnosed at some point in their lives. This means that we all have a personal need to understand depression. Yet, it is a hard topic to get our minds around, even for students and clinicians, because there are so many different models of depression. Lay persons have an added difficulty because, when the diagnosis comes, they are not in a good place to start researching the condition. They are in a vulnerable state of mind and will tend to hold on to the first explanation they are given. But the first explanation may not be the right one for the person involved. In addition, both lay persons and clinicians have trouble getting a handle on depression because the field of psychiatry is complicated and often controversial. The dominant model, the biopsychiatric model, has much to offer, but at the same time it tends to overshadow other options. This can make it hard to put biological models in perspective and to fully appreciate available alternatives.

This means that at the time of diagnosis both lay persons and clinicians have two problems—they have to deal with the very personal issues that stimulated the diagnosis and they have to navigate the social and cultural controversies surrounding the diagnostic category and current standards of treatment. My goal in this book is to use scholarship in psychiatry, the humanities, and cultural studies to help people prepare in advance for times of crisis. I approach depression through a comparative lens that contrasts the leading biopsychiatric model with a host of other models that have been prominent historically, across cultures, and in our own time. By putting this comparative work together in a single text, students can get a better handle on the multiple ways to understand and frame depression. They will also get a chance to use narrative theory to work through what it means to have so many ways to understand depression. I find that narrative theory provides invaluable tools for understanding the multiple models of depression and for helping people make choices regarding which model (or combination of models) might be most valuable for them.

I end the book with a discussion of clinical encounters that highlight how people navigate multiple choices and options in depression recovery. This chapter looks at stories of depression that have shown up in fiction, creative non-fiction, and qualitative research. These narratives reveal the tremendous diversity of recovery paths for depression. They show that a deep awareness of the diverse possibilities of understanding and responding to depression can prepare the mind for utilizing recovery tools from a variety of sources. Insight into this diversity is invaluable for helping people take care of themselves in times of depression, and also for clinicians and recovery allies who are charged with the task of helping others.

ACKNOWLEDGMENTS

Professor Lennard Davis made this book possible. He had the wisdom and insight to develop a series that explores complicated topics at the interface of biology and culture. Without his inspiration, and of course without the patience and support of my family, this book would never have happened. I would also like to thank Leah Babb-Rosenfeld and the staff at Routledge for excellent editorial and production assistance. The pre-publication reviewers they orchestrated, including Allan Horwitz at Rutgers New Brunswick and Ronald Pies at SUNY Upstate, were particularly helpful in improving the manuscript. In addition, I would like to thank the many students I have worked with at New York University's Gallatin School of Individualized Study for helping me work through these topics. I have been exploring these issues with them for the last several years. For earlier versions of material in Chapters 2 and 5, please see *Narrative Psychiatry: How Stories Can Shape Clinical Encounters* published by Johns Hopkins Press.

INTRODUCTION

We live in an era of depression. The World Health Organization estimates that depression affects 121 million people across the globe. It is the fourth leading contributor to the global disease burden, and by the year 2020 it will be the second leading contributor. Moreover, the experience of depression can be intensely painful. Andrew Solomon, in his memoir *The Noonday Demon: An Atlas of Depression*, compares his experience of depression to that of a strong and dignified oak tree, persistently and maliciously conquered by a parasitic vine. Melancholia wrapped itself around him, ugly and sure, until his life was gradually asphyxiated: "I knew that the sun was rising and setting, but little of its light reached me. I felt myself sagging under what was much stronger than I" (Solomon 2001, 18). At its worst, this kind of agony can lead to suicide, killing approximately 850,000 persons every year, and beyond those directly affected, the morbidity and mortality of depression deeply impacts friends, co-workers, children, parents, and loved ones.

Despite the extensive suffering caused by depression, there remains considerable debate about how to understand it. In the West, depression is increasingly seen through the frames of biomedicine. "Broken brains" and "chemical imbalances" have become the popular but crude catch-alls for a vast and ever growing body of biomedical research that attempts to link depression and depressive episodes to our bodies, our neural synapses, and our brains. In spite of the prevalence of the biomedical model, however, depression continues to be understood

1

through a variety of other models, including psychoanalytic, cognitive-behavioral, existential/humanist, family, political, creative, spiritual, and biopsychsosocial models.

Depression: Integrating Science, Culture, and Humanities reviews the varied and multiple models of depression and not only shows the many ways depression is understood today but also how it has been understood across time and cultures. Being aware of the differing models is illuminating—what they look like, where and when they formed—but an awareness of the multiple models of depression also leads to an important set of questions: Which of these models is "best?" Which comes closest to the "truth" of depression? Can one model, or a combination of models, offer a "solution" to depression? And what does a "solution" for depression really mean? If depression is reaching epidemic and grossly debilitating proportions, as reports suggest, these questions need to be urgently considered, and this book offers a theoretical and conceptual toolkit with which to do so.

Part One, 'The Facts" starts with "What We Teach Our Doctors," a chapter that reviews current psychiatric textbook presentations of biomedical and epidemiological research surrounding depression. Chapter 2, "What We Also Know," extends this discussion to consider an array of other contemporary models used to understand depression.

Part Two, "Historical and Cultural Perspectives," puts our current approaches to depression in broader perspective. Chapter 3, "Western History," reviews historical dimensions of depression. Chapter 4, "Cultural Context," considers anthropological perspectives on depression across cultures and unpacks the many ways that the transnational pharmaceutical industry has transformed the culture of depression in Japan and the U.S.

Part Three, "Theoretical and Clinical Concerns," considers the challenges and possibilities of having so many models of depression. Chapter 5, "What We May Never Know," uses narrative theory to help us navigate the multiple models of depression and to ask what we can do in the face of such multiplicity. Chapter 6, "Clinical Encounters," considers the practical implications of the material we have discussed. This chapter looks closely at a fictional portrayal of depression, recent memoirs of depression, and outcome of studies devoted to depression for guidance on how to live with, and through, depression.

PART I
THE FACTS

1 What We Teach Our Doctors

Depression, we can say for certain, has become the subject of extensive scientific research. This research is the mainstay of contemporary medical and psychiatric understandings of depression, and it makes up the vast bulk of what we teach our doctors about depression. We need a thorough understanding of this scientific research because when we go to the doctor with complaints of depression our doctor will use it to make sense of our concerns. In addition, although this research can be controversial, it contains invaluable insights and information on depression.

To access contemporary medical and psychiatric approaches to depression, some of the best places to turn to are psychiatric textbooks—which distill a vast amount of scientific research for medical students, general physicians, and psychiatric specialists (as well as psychologists, social workers, nurses, and counselors). This does not mean there is a one-to-one relationship between psychiatric textbooks and what particular clinicians may think. Textbook knowledge is further developed and refined by clinical experience, mentorship with senior clinicians, conference meetings, seminars, continuing education, and further reading of books and journals. But, nonetheless, psychiatric textbooks do provide the basic frame from which our healthcare workers think about depression. For this reason, we start our study of depression with an overview of contemporary psychiatric textbook presentations. Along the way, we will also discuss some of the scientific controversies surrounding this material.

Textbooks of psychiatry generally organize their presentation of depression with sections devoted to *diagnosis, epidemiology, pathophysiology, and treatment*.[1] We follow this outline and our focus will be on "major depressive disorder"—or as it is often called "major depression" or more simply "depression." Major depression is a subset of a broader class of conditions known as "mood disorders." As a group, mood disorders share a "disturbance of mood" (or sustained emotion) as their most prominent feature. Major depression is the mood disorder characterized by episodes of depressive mood that may occur one or more times during a person's life.

Diagnosis

In the United States, psychiatry has strived to produce a rigorously descriptive criterion for depression. The *Diagnostic and Statistical Manual IV-TR (DSM IV-TR)*, psychiatry's primary diagnostic guide, provides the following classification for a major depressive episode:

DSM-IV-TR Diagnostic Criteria

Major Depressive Episode

A. Five (or more) of the following symptoms have been present during the same 2-week period and represent a change from previous functioning; at least one of the symptoms is either (1) depressed mood or (2) loss of interest or pleasure.

    (1) depressed mood;
    (2) markedly diminished interest or pleasure;
    (3) significant weight loss when not dieting or weight gain, or decrease or increase in appetite;
    (4) insomnia or hypersomnia;
    (5) psychomotor agitation or retardation;
    (6) fatigue or loss of energy;

(7) feelings of worthlessness or excessive or inappropriate guilt;

(8) diminished ability to think or concentrate, or indecisiveness;

(9) recurrent thoughts of death or suicide.

B. The symptoms do not meet criteria for a Mixed Episode (of manic and depressive symptoms).

C. The symptoms cause significant distress or impairment in social, occupational, or other important areas of functioning.

D. The symptoms are not due to the direct physiological effects of a substance (e.g. a drug of abuse, a medication) or a general medical condition (e.g. hypothyroidism).

E. The symptoms are not better accounted for by bereavement, i.e., after the loss of a loved one, the symptoms persist for longer than two months and are characterized by marked functional impairment, morbid preoccupation with worthlessness, suicidal ideation, psychotic symptoms, or psychomotor retardation.

Adapted from *Diagnostic and Statistical Manual of Mental Disorders* (American Psychiatric Association 2000)

Textbooks of psychiatry use these criteria, and they organize their descriptions of *DSM-IV* symptoms by dividing them into three categories: 1) emotional symptoms; 2) cognitive symptoms; and 3) vegetative symptoms.

The cardinal *emotional symptoms* are depressed mood and loss of pleasure. These emotional symptoms are so important to the criteria of major depression that without at least one of these symptoms the diagnosis cannot be made. Depressed mood is a profound sadness that goes beyond everyday blues in longevity (greater than two weeks) and intensity (severe enough to interfere with functioning). This sadness is often accompanied by irritability, anxiety, discouragement, or an overall feeling or lassitude and heaviness. In clear cases, people will bemoan their situation on interview, and they will seem sad and tearful as well. They may cry profusely, their facial musculature may sag, they may have a pained look on their face with a furrowed or pinched brow, and they may be slouched or hunched over in the chair. All of this can make others, including the psychiatrist, feel sad as well.

Lack of pleasure, or anhedonia, is the other cardinal mood symptom of depression. Anhedonic patients lose interest in former attachments and curiosity for new possibilities in life. They take limited pleasure in their activities; little arouses them—even sexual attraction can lose its appeal—and in general they must force themselves to do things they previously enjoyed. As a result, they often go about their day lifeless and desolate.

Prominent *cognitive symptoms* of major depression include difficulty concentrating, indecision, and memory problems. People with depression often find it hard to focus and complain of confusion, dullness, and forgetfulness. They describe themselves as being in a fog or like they are under water. They have trouble remembering where they put things or what they are planning to do. Simple tasks such as reading can be excruciating, and they are often forced to read the same page over and over again to understand it. Decision making can also be difficult, and even basic choices can become overwhelming. For example, in severe cases people experiencing a depressive episode find it impossible to decide what to wear or what to do in the day.

Other cognitive symptoms include negative thoughts centering on themes of worthlessness, guilt, and shame. People with depression often blame themselves for their problems, the problems of others, and even the woes of the world. They may loudly berate themselves, confessing and accusing themselves of the worst sins and derelictions. Their self-esteem and self-worth is often very low, and they may see themselves as having never done anything of value. When they look over their lives, they may seem blind to accomplishments and aware only of misdeeds and shortcomings. This can become magnified to heinous proportions, even to the point that the person feels evil or somehow rotten to the core. They may ruminate about their failings and defects, and they may repeat their gloomy predictions for the future in an interminable litany.

For many, suicidal thoughts can be a constant preoccupation. Suicidal thoughts may be passive in that people may wish to die of some disease or accident without any intent to bring their own demise. Or they may be active, in that people may make conscious plans to hang or shoot themselves, jump from tall buildings, or overdose on dangerous medicines. These thoughts come partly from the pain of depression and partly because of deep pessimism about the future. The risk of a suicide may be highest when the depressive episode starts to lift. In early recovery, while still feeling worthless and hopeless, people may have enough energy to carry out suicidal plans that they only thought about before.

In a small percentage of cases, cognitive disturbances become so severe that psychiatrists use the term "psychotic depression" to describe them. The most common psychotic depression involves extreme negative thoughts that devolve into frank delusions or hallucinations. A delusion is a fixed unshakeable belief that others find improbable or fantastic. Commonly, delusions in depression magnify other symptoms. Guilt may become extreme, and people may confess to unspeakable, impossible sins. For example, they may believe that they have poisoned their children, or that they have caused world pollution, hunger, and war. They may believe they are condemned to hell, or that they are possessed by Satan. They may feel deservedly persecuted, that their neighbors or co-workers talk about them, or that the police survey them with hidden cameras. They may have delusions of poverty and destitution or may believe themselves to have a terminal disease or be near death. Auditory hallucinations, when they occur, generally reflect delusions. Voices may accuse people of evil deeds or may announce their execution. Visual or olfactory hallucinations, though rare, can also occur.

Psychiatrists refer to *vegetative symptoms* as those disturbances that seem most embodied, such as disturbances of sleep, appetite, energy level, and sexuality. All of these can increase or decrease, but for the most part they go down in depression. Decreased sleep, or insomnia, is a common sleep problem in depression. People have trouble falling asleep, or more typically, they wake up in the middle of the night or early in the morning and having trouble getting back to sleep. During these waking hours people can experience depressive ruminations and worries that they cannot escape. On the other hand, some people with depression complain of hypersomnia, with a tendency to sleep much longer than usual, or to take naps throughout the day.

Energy levels in depression are often very low, with people complaining of feeling tired, fatigued, lifeless, or drained. But for some people, energy levels go up—with an excess of nervous energy, mild agitation, restlessness, and hand wringing. Appetite can also go up or down. Most commonly people lose their appetite, and for many this means significant weight loss. In these cases, food may lose its taste and may even leave people feeling nauseated when they try to eat. By contrast, some people find themselves hungry all the time, using food in an attempt to soothe themselves to the point that they can put on considerable weight. Finally, libido is usually much diminished, with people losing most, if not all, interest in sex. But occasionally, it goes the other way around and people find themselves constantly turning to sex or masturbation for comfort.

Epidemiology

Psychiatric epidemiologists study the rates of psychiatric conditions in populations. Epidemiologic research helps us understand the extent and burden of depression as well as social and demographic factors that may cause or contribute to depression. Psychiatric epidemiologists commonly report rates in terms of *prevalence*—which is a percentage calculated by dividing the number of cases (per unit of time) by the population.

Influential studies of major depression in the U.S., Europe, and Australia find a one-year prevalence of depression somewhere between 3% and 10% of the population. Over a lifetime, the prevalence ranges from 5% to 17% of the population (Rihmer and Angst 2009, 1648). The wide range in these numbers comes from the variability of populations along with the diagnostic reliability of the instruments used. Still, if we take an average of these numbers, we can get a fair approximation of the epidemiology of depression in Western countries —7% one-year prevalence and 12% lifetime prevalence.

A well-respected study in the U.S. found that major depression was the most common psychiatric condition causing significant morbidity. Major depression tied with phobia in terms of one-year prevalence (at 7.1%) and was significantly higher than the next most common disorder, which was alcohol abuse (4.7%) (Narrow and Rubio-Stipec 2009, 767). The extent and severity of depression was made particularly poignant by the Global Burden of Disease study, sponsored by the World Health Organization (WHO) and the World Bank. This study looked not only at disease prevalence but also at the extent to which disease caused disability. For developed regions, the study found that major depression was the *leading psychiatric cause of disability*. Furthermore, the study found that major depression caused more years lived with disability than any other disease—including medical diseases such as diabetes, cerebrovascular disease, cancer, and traffic accidents (p. 769).

Epidemiologic studies also reveal consistent sociodemographic patterns for depression. The mean age of onset for major depression is generally in the late 20s. After that depression tends to be recurrent across the life span. Occurrence with other psychiatric conditions is common. Women are twice as likely as men to suffer from depression. Married people suffer depression less often than their single or divorced cohorts. People who are unemployed or have low socioeconomic status have increased rates of depression, and low-income single mothers have an especially high risk. Race and ethnicity are thought to be risk factors particularly when combined with socioeconomic factors. In addition, several studies have found increasing prevalence of depression over the last half century. However, this finding is controversial, and others argue that the increase is due to heightened cultural awareness and preoccupation with depression as a condition (see Chapter 4 for further discussion of this concern).

Epidemiological studies of risk factors have focused extensively on familial patterns and stress. A family history of major depression increases the risk for depression, and a family history also increases the risk of more severe depression. Twin studies and adoption studies point to an at least partial genetic component to these family trends. Estimates of the monozygotic-to-dizygotic ratio have found as high as 4:1 increased prevalence in monozygotic compared to dizygotic twins. Stress is also a well-documented epidemiological risk factor for depression. Early childhood traumas and negative life events increase the risk of depression—particularly child abuse (physical, sexual, and neglect) and the loss of significant other. In adults, too, stressful life events in family, work, health, and finances increase the risk of depression.

The link between loss, negative life events, and stress is the leading explanation for increased depression among women and lower socioeconomic groups. Increased prejudice, disadvantage, and hardship faced by lower status groups yield considerably increased stress and therefore increased depression. However, there is also evidence that those with a family history of depression are more vulnerable to stressful events than others. It seems from this evidence that there is a spiraling, and bidirectional, effect of depression and stress. Persons who are depressed for whatever reason have increased difficulty managing life challenges—obtaining and maintaining work, relationships, self-care, etc. These can all lead to increased stress, loss, negative life events, and lower socioeconomic status (Williams and Neighbors 2006). This same spiraling relationship between stress and vulnerability shows up in recent pathophysiological studies of depression, which suggests that individual genetic predisposition interacts with psychological and social factors.

Pathophysiology

In recent years, the vast bulk of causal research in psychiatry has focused on a search for biological abnormalities in depression. Genetic vulnerabilities were discussed in the last section. In this section research on neurochemical and neuroanatomical pathology will be considered.

Extensive neurochemical research has centered on the "monoamine theory" of depression. The term monoamine refers to the neurotransmitters (chemical messengers) norepinephrine, serotonin, and dopamine. The theory evolved because of the effects of medications on depression. By the 1950s, there were several medications observed either to trigger depressive symptoms or to reduce them. For example, iproniazid (first used for tuberculosis) was found to decrease depressive symptoms and was known to be a monoamine oxidase inhibitor. By inhibiting the oxidation (or breakdown) of monamines, iproniazid effectively increased the amount of monoamines available for neurotransmission. Similarly, imipramine, the first antidepressant widely used, also worked on the monoamines. Julius Axelrod won the Nobel prize for his research showing that imipramine and similar medications blocked the reuptake of monoamines in the synapse (the space between nerve endings). Blocking the reuptake of monoamines also effectively increases their availability in the synapse. By the 1960s and 1970s studies such as these led to a wide consensus known as "the monoamine hypothesis" that depression was caused by a deficit of norepinephrine and serotonin.

This period of consensus around the monoamine hypothesis is the scientific background for the popular use of the phrase "chemical imbalance" to explain depression. But over the past 15 years the monoamine hypothesis has lost ground in scientific circles. Studies of norepinephrine and serotonin have not reliably shown depleted levels, and evidence for a primary neurochemical dysfunction has been lacking (Delgado and Moreno 2006, 111).

Increasingly, research into depression has moved from the neuro-chemical level to the neuroanatomical level. Neurochemical factors may be important, but many argue they must be understood in relation to larger brain structures and neuro-circuits that modulate emotion and cognition. Brain scans—computed tomography (CT), magnetic resonance imaging (MRI), positron emission tomography (PET), and functional magnetic resonance imaging (fMRI)—have shown that brain anatomy is grossly normal in most individuals diagnosed with depression. Focal abnormalities, similar to those seen in neurological disorders, are not found. However, more subtle findings in areas of the brain have been suggestive of neuropathology in depression. There is evidence of cellular changes in the areas of the brain associated throughout the frontolimbic system (a neuro-circuit from the frontal region to the limbic region that is thought to be the emotional circuit of the brain).

An area of intense interest has been the use of postmortem comput-erized cell-counting techniques to study depression. These studies, which are considerably more sensitive than traditional microscopic techniques, report abnormalities in cell size and density in the frontolimbic system (Rajkowska 2006, 179). The abnormalities are cumulative (they increase with increased length of depression) and they involve both neuronal cells and glial cells. Glial cells give support to the neuronal cells both by providing architectural structure and by digesting debris and toxins. The cause of cumulative neuronal and glial cell pathology is unclear, but researchers hypothesize that it is related to stress induced changes and the failure of the brain in depressed patients to repair itself. This damage and impaired healing hypothesis is supported by data showing that brain structures can be damaged by stress, and the finding that the brain has the capacity to partially regenerate itself through neuroplasticity and cellular resilience. Both brain imaging studies and postmortem studies provide evidence that people with depression have impairments in neuroplasticity and cellular resilience. This suggests that depression may be caused in part by increased vulnerability to stress and impaired healing from stress (Singh, Quiroz, Gould, Zarate, and Manji 2006, 198).

Peter Kramer, a practicing psychiatrist and popular science writer, put together these research findings into a narrative that provides a clear biological explanation for depression. For Kramer, the neuro-anatomical research results effectively "embodied" his clinical experience of working with patients. Neuropathology showed neuronal and glial cells are "weakened, disorganized, [and] disconnected," which reminded him of how his patients seemed to him (Kramer 2005, 53). In addition, the severity of his patient's problems seemed biological to him, way beyond problems in living. "[This is] not normal variation, one way of being a human rather than another. The changes look like brain damage—abnormal pathology" (p. 53). The specifics of vulnerability, damage, and impaired repair matched Kramer's clinical experience. "At every level, from social circumstance, to psychological take on the self, to brain chemistry, to cellular anatomy, the depressive lacks support. In the brain and in daily life, the core deficits in depression are identical: vulnerability to harm, failures of resilience" (p. 57). Kramer concludes that in both the clinics and in neuroanatomical study, depression is a disease of "fragility, brittleness, lack of resilience and failure to heal. Depression is chronic and progressive, with each episode—perhaps each day!—leaving damage in its wake. Depression is not normal variation; it is pathology—and risk of further harm" (p. 61).

Scientific Controversy

Scientific critique of psychiatric research and popular presentations such as Kramer's tend to focus on the problem of *diagnostic bracket creep*. Diagnostic bracket creep refers to diagnostic categories that start small, with disease criteria relevant for a very small percentage of the population, and then gradually expand to include more and more of the population. Psychiatric researchers Allan V. Horwitz and Jerome Wakefield effectively use this critique in their influential book *The Loss of Sadness: How Psychiatry Transformed Normal Sorrow into Depressive Disorder* (Horwitz and Wakefield 2007). Horwitz and Wakefield argue that psychiatric research on depression is scientifically flawed because the *DSM* fails to adequately distinguish between two types of depression: normal sadness and major depression (p. 6).[2] These two types of depression share similar symptoms: "sadness, insomnia, social withdrawal, loss of appetite, lack of interest in usual activities, and so on" (p. 6). However, for Horwitz and Wakefield, there is a clear distinction between them: normal sadness has an environmental cause and major depression does not.

Normal sadness is associated with environmental traumas of "loss or other painful circumstances that seemed to be the obvious causes of distress" (p. 6). Normal sadness is common and not pathological. It is a normal reaction to difficult situations. People with normal sadness may need support and help, but they are not ill. By contrast, major depression is depression without a cause. Major depression occurs with no appropriate external cause for the sadness, and the reasons are thus considered to be internal to the individual. For Horwitz and Wakefield, major depression is a rare medical disorder associated with pathological dysfunction or defect that tends to be long-lasting and recurrent. Their work articulates the widespread concern that the failure to adequately separate normal sadness from major depression has led to an epidemic of depressive diagnoses. Out-patient diagnosis of depression has grown by "300% between 1987 and 1997," and for many critics of psychiatry, the bulk of this increased diagnosis of depression is misdiagnosis.

Horwitz and Wakefield take us into the technical details of the *DSM* to show how the diagnostic inflation and bracket creep occurred. In general, they find no real problem with the descriptive criteria for Major Depression, but they see a glaring error with regard to *DSM* exclusion criteria. The *DSM* excludes the diagnosis of Major Depression if the symptoms can be "better accounted for by Bereavement, i.e., after the loss of a loved one" (p. 8). This logic of the Bereavement shows how intense experiences of sadness can be normal and appropriate, but the problem is that Bereavement only scratches the surface of negative life events that can make depression understandable and appropriate. Additional life events include romantic betrayal, failure at work or school, life-threatening illness in oneself or in a loved one, enduring humiliation after disgraceful behavior, etc. "[Depressive] reactions even when quite intense due to the severity of the experience, are surely part of normal human nature" (p. 9).

Horwitz and Wakefield argue that *DSM-III* framers fell into this kind of bracket creep because they were working in a time of crisis for psychiatry. During the 1970s, popular critiques of psychiatry, the field's theoretical fragmentation, and its diagnostic unreliability left "psychiatry's claim to scientific status" at risk (p. 100). Psychiatry's "legitimacy as a medical field seemed in jeopardy," and *DSM-III* framers responded with a "largely decontextualized, symptom-based criteria ... [designed] to bolster the scientific credentials of the profession" (pp. 100, 103). But the framers went too far. "In the urgent quest for reliability," they "inadvertently" failed to develop a diagnostic system that included appropriate contextual exclusions (p. 103). Once this flawed diagnostic system spread to the community, psychiatry unintentionally initiated a "massive pathologization of normal sadness" (p. 103).

For Horwitz and Wakefield, the solution to bracket creep is to correct it with better scientific criteria. Over-diagnosis can be corrected by expanding the next *DSM*'s exclusion criteria to include a variety of contextual exclusions beyond Bereavement. An additional diagnostic category can be created for "nondisordered but treatable" conditions. These changes would allow much more "watchful waiting" in clinical settings rather than the immediate use of the diagnosis of major depression (p. 223).

The psychiatric rejoinder to the "loss of sadness" critique is that it risks under-diagnosing a potentially fatal disease. The exclusion of "normal sadness" would result in the opposite problem—many people with very "real disease" would not be diagnosed. As a result, rather than over-diagnosis, we would have under-diagnosis—particularly in cultures where there is tremendous stigma against mental illness. In addition, putting loss of sadness critiques in action would force clinicians to make value judgments about "appropriate" contexts for major depression rather than basing their decisions on the descriptions of symptoms. Removing these kinds of value judgments from the diagnostic criteria is exactly what the scientifically framed *DSM-III* tried to do in the first place.

For most psychiatrists, the issue is not the occurrence of stressful life events; the issue is whether or not the stress turns into diagnosable depression. As psychiatrist Derek Bolton put it in his review of Horwitz and Wakefield's work, "So far as I can see, clinicians have little use for the distinction between normal and abnormal depression except in the sense that normal may be used to mean: self-limiting, unlikely to carry risk, and no need to treat" (Bolton 2009). Bolton and like-minded clinicians do not use the occurrence of loss as a guide for treatment. The key issue is whether the patient is in significant pain or is at risk of harm to self or others. "Contextualising is less the issue: harm, risk and need to treat are" (Bolton 2009).

In later chapters we will get a chance to consider the theoretical and cultural issues surrounding controversies in psychiatry. But for now, it is enough to see how the "loss of sadness" critique is a serious challenge to contemporary psychiatric research and at the same time will not be persuasive for many in the psychiatric community. This controversial aspect of psychiatric research will likely remain for some time.

Treatment

Psychiatric textbooks consider a number of treatment options for depression, particularly biological, cognitive-behavioral, psychoanalytic, and biopsychosocial treatments. Consistent with recent neuroscience research on depression, most textbooks of psychiatry emphasize and give the most attention to biological treatments. This chapter reviews these biological treatments, and in the next chapter we will discuss additional options.

Electroconvulsive therapy (ECT) is the longest running biological therapy for depression. First introduced in 1938, ECT involves placing electrodes on the patient's skull and running sufficient electrical current to induce a seizure. Patients with depression usually receive six to nine treatments spaced two to three times per week. The mechanism of action is unknown, but neurochemical theories have been proposed and extensively studied (Nobler and Sackeim 2006, 319). Psychiatric textbooks commonly report that ECT is highly effective, with up to 80% response rates (Andreason and Black 2006, 162). However ECT is not commonly used today. Public opinion is often negative, and there are very real side effects to ECT. Current treatment protocols have

reduced the physical impact of the seizure by giving the patient sedatives
and muscle relaxants, but there remains a host of cognitive side effects,
including disorientation, antegrade amnesia, and retrograde amnesia
(Joska and Stein 2010, 22).

The complications of ECT mean that antidepressant medications
are the mainstay of biological treatments. The mechanism of antidepressant efficacy is also not fully known, but as we discussed, the
drugs are known to affect monoamine (norepinephrine and serotonin)
levels in the brain. Textbooks generally provide a rational for antidepressants through this hypothesis and through popular notions of
"chemical imbalance" even though the monoamine hypothesis is now
dated from a scientific standpoint. Andreason and Black explain
antidepressant action in their book *Introductory Textbook of Psychiatry*
this way: "These drugs are all thought to work by altering levels of
various neurotransmitters at crucial nerve terminals in the central
nervous system" (Andreason and Black 2006, 161).

There are a variety of different antidepressants available, and the
drugs are usually grouped in terms of their activity at neuroreceptors.
The tricyclics (imipramine, desipramine, and amitriptyline), which
were the first widely used group of antidepressants, block the reuptake of both norepinephrine and serotonin. The effects of tricyclics
(TCAs) on monoamines are not specific, however, and these medications have effects on a variety of other neurotransmitters throughout
the brain. This causes a range of troublesome side effects such as dry
mouth, constipation, blurred vision, fatigue, low blood pressure, cardiac
arrhythmias, increased appetite, and weight gain. Apart from these
side effects, textbook authors can be very optimistic about the positive
effects of these drugs. As one text puts it, "Overall, the response rate
for the TCAs is 80% in non-psychotic patients who have a primary
diagnosis of major depressive disorder . . ." (Potter, Padich, Rudorfer,
and Krishnan 2006, 254).

The antidepressants in the other major class are known as the
selective serotonin reuptake inhibitors (SSRIs). The breakout
medication from this group, Prozac (fluoxetine), became a blockbuster
during the 1990s. Similar medications, Paxil (paroxetine) and Zoloft
(sertraline), were also best sellers. More recent medications in this class
include Celexa (citalopram) and Lexapro (escitalopram). The SSRIs

are also reported in textbooks to be very effective, with a commonly cited response rate of 60% to 70% (Shelton and Lester 2006, 269). Since they are more selective in their action, they have reduced side effects compared to TCAs. But the SSRIs do have side effect problems. The two most troublesome are sexual dysfunction and suicide risk. Common sexual side effects include decreased libido, decreased erection or labial engorgement, and difficulty reaching orgasm. This occurs in up to half of people taking these medications and can be a persistent problem for around 15% (Shelton and Lester 2006, 274). The increased risk of suicidal ideation and suicide attempts has been particularly controversial in the scientific literature. When the issue was reviewed by the Food and Drug Administration (FDA) in 2004 the FDA found sufficient evidence to issue a public health advisory. The FDA recommended close observation of the emergence of suicidal thoughts and behaviors in all patients treated with SSRIs.

Additional antidepressants introduced after the SSRIs include Effexor (venlafaxine) and Cymbalta (duloxetine), which are newer medications that selectively affect both serotonin and norepinephrine. There is also Wellbutrin (bupropion) which primarily affects norepinephrine. All of these medications have relatively similar side effect profiles as the SSRIs with some increased risk of high blood pressure (for Effexor) and seizures (for Wellbutrin).

All classes of antidepressants introduced to date are thought to have very similar overall effectiveness and speed of onset. They differ primarily in pharmacology, drug interactions, side effects, and dosing schedules. Standard treatment recommendations suggest beginning with an SSRI since they have relatively few side effects and generally require low doses. Effectiveness usually begins in a few weeks, and a full trial lasts from four to eight weeks. If there is no response in four weeks, the dose can be increased or switched to a different drug (generally from a different class). If there is still no response, most textbooks recommend adding a second or sometimes a third medication to augment the first. These augmenting drugs can be additional antidepressants, or drugs from other classes, such as mood stabilizers, antipsychotics, thyroid medications, or antianxiety drugs. The use of multiple drug "cocktails" for depression is a common clinical practice, but there is limited research to support it. Most augmentation strategies use medications off-label in an effort to find a combination that will be effective.

Before leaving antidepressants, it is important to consider the scientific controversy surrounding these drugs. Another scientific controversy around antidepressants—in addition to the question of suicide risk—is the question of overtreatment. This concern is related to the loss of sadness critique. If major depression is over-diagnosed, then it is also overtreated with medications. As Horwitz and Wakefield point out, "antidepressant medications, such as Prozac, Paxil, Zoloft, and Effexor, are now among the largest selling prescription drugs of any sort. Their use among adults nearly tripled between 1988 and 2000" (Horwitz and Wakefield, 2007, 4). Antidepressant medication has become so pervasive that in any given month "10% of women and 4% of men now use these drugs" (p. 4). In addition, "during the 1990s, spending for antidepressants increased by 600% in the United States, exceeding $7 billion annually by the year 2000" (pp. 4–5). All of this is deeply controversial, and a host of critiques inside and outside psychiatry are concerned about the overuse of antidepressants.

The other issue that has been particularly controversial in the scientific literature is the question of therapeutic efficacy for the anti-depressants. Textbooks give favorable outcome numbers, as we have seen, but critical scientific reviewers have been much less positive. Many critical scientists reviewing the data found that these medications are not better than placebo (a sugar pill) in treating depression (see, for example, Breggin 1994, 65; Fisher and Fisher 1996). In 1998, psychologists Irving Kirsch and Guy Sapirstein did an extensive meta-analysis of the efficacy literature. They looked at 19 double-blind studies involving over 2,000 patients. Kirsch and Sapirstein concluded that inactive placebos produced 75% of the SSRIs' efficacy. Not only that, they also speculated that the other 25% came largely from non-specific side effects. As Kirsch and Sapirstein put it, most researchers were "listening to Prozac but hearing placebo" (Kirsch and Sapirstein 1998).

This efficacy controversy continues to this day. Some people champion SSRIs; others believe these medications hardly work at all. So far, there are no signs of resolution on the horizon. After Kirsch and Sapirstein published their meta-analysis, their findings were disputed in the medical literature by Klein and Quitkin (Klein 1998,

Quitkin, Rabkin, Gerald, Davis, and Klein 2000). Kirsch, with several colleagues, responded to Klein and Quitkin with a follow-up study that reasserted their findings (Kirsch, Moore, Scoboria, and Nicholls 2002). The popular press also picked up the placebo controversy and ran a series of stories with titles such as "Maybe It's All in Your Head," "Make-Believe Medicine," "Antidepressants: Hype or Help," and "Misguided Medicine: A Stunning Finding about Antidepressants is Being Ignored." The most extensive of these popular press stories ran in the *Washington Post* and was titled "Against Depression: A Sugar Pill Is Hard to Beat" (Vedantam 2002). *Post* reporter S. Vedantam emphasized the placebo side of the controversy, but researchers Brandon Gaudiano and James Herbert disputed Vedantam's main claims (Gaudiano and Herbert 2003). They warned that the recent media flurry was in danger of overhyping the "power" of placebo and the "powerlessness" of antidepressants such as Prozac. Going the other direction, psychiatrist Joanna Moncrieff reviewed the research evidence and concluded that "SSRIs have only minor effects compared with placebo" (Moncrieff 2009, 163).

Beyond efficacy, the related controversial scientific question regarding SSRIs involves the question of explanation. Why does an antidepressant such as Prozac work (if we believe that they do work, that is)? Here again, science gives contradictory answers. Some argue vociferously that SSRIs "work" because they treat a specific biological disease. To use the popular culture version of biopsychiatry, antidepressants treat depression the way insulin treats diabetes. The diabetes analogy runs as follows. Treatment of diabetes requires insulin replacement; treatment of depression therefore requires "chemical balance." Even in more sophisticated neuroscience models, the basic idea is the same—antidepressants work through treating some form of brain dysfunction.

Others argue just as vociferously against the broken brain analogy. For some, SSRIs work (if they do work) simply because they are psychic stimulants. SSRIs work on the same neurotransmitter systems as other stimulants (such as cocaine and amphetamines), and thus they are similar mood brighteners and psychic energizers. Sigmund Freud described the stimulant effects of cocaine as far back as 1884. He found that cocaine produced:

> Exhilaration and lasting euphoria, which in no way differs from the normal euphoria of the healthy person . . . . You perceive an increase of self-control and possess more vitality and capacity for work . . . In other words, you are simply normal, and it is hard to believe that you are under the influence of any drug . . . . Long intensive mental or physical work is performed without fatigue . . . The result is enjoyed without any of the unpleasant after effects that follow exhilaration brought about by alcohol . . .
>
> (quoted in Breggin 1994, 116)

Over one hundred years later, former cocaine abusers report that Prozac gives them the same feeling as a mild dose of cocaine:

> So long as I didn't do too much coke, if I just did a few lines, I would feel in a good mood. It was only when I did too much or if I smoked it or shot it up instead of snorting lines that I would feel really racy and strung out. Prozac is like the milder effect, like just a line or two.
>
> (Glenmullen 2000, 213)

If we understand SSRIs as working like a mild stimulant, there is no need to hypothesize about it treating a specific "mental disease" or a "chemical imbalance." SSRIs just produce the stimulant effect of speed. It would do so on anyone.

In *The Myth of the Chemical Cure: A Critique of Psychiatric Drug Treatment*, psychiatric researcher Joanna Moncrieff agrees with critics that these drugs do not have anything like a disease-specific efficacy (Moncrieff 2009). However, she does not find good evidence for SSRIs being stimulants either. Moncrieff finds some evidence that a "single dose of an SSRI might produce a slight stimulant effect," but this evidence is not statistically significant nor did it bear out over the longer term (p. 163). Indeed, Moncrieff found more evidence in the other direction, that in the longer term SSRIs can be associated with sedating effects and mild cognitive impairment. This is further complicated by evidence that SSRIs can produce an "activating effect," with impaired sleep, restlessness, and agitation (p. 164). These activating effects seem different from classical stimulants. SSRI activation effects do not bring with them a sense of well-being associated with classical stimulants, and may be unpleasant enough to lead to suicidal thinking in rare cases.

Moncrieff argues that we do not really know the effects SSRIs have on people. Based on what she found in her review, she does not believe SSRIs have a role in the treatment of major depression. Her conclusion in this regard is in direct contradiction to that of the psychiatric textbooks. As she puts it, "The SSRIs produce no effects that look likely to be useful in depression. They cause unpleasant agitation in a proportion of patients and, although it is difficult to prove conclusively, an increase in suicidal and violent tendencies may be associated with this effect. Therefore, I can think of no good reason to prescribe them at all" (p. 172).

Regrettably, uncertainties such as these are not uncommon in healthcare, and there are many medications whose action we do not fully understand and their use is controversial. At present, clinical opinion regarding antidepressants remains favorable, and many patients are very appreciative of their effect. Although it is only a study of one, I will add that in my experience as a psychiatrist, I too have found that antidepressant medications are often helpful for people struggling with depressive symptoms. They are hardly a panacea, however. They are not for everyone, their side effects are real, and, as we will see in Chapter 4, the cultural hype around them can drown out other options. But, still, they do seem to have a role to play in dealing with depression.

Conclusion

Scientific research has yielded important and extensive findings on depression. Moreover, scientific psychiatry has yielded the most widely researched and commonly used treatment for depression—antidepressant medications. No consideration of depression would be complete without taking this research seriously. On the other hand, it would be a mistake to close down our curiosity here. Not only is this research controversial, there is also a vast literature left to explore. Depression has a long history and has yielded itself to a wide variety of approaches and insights.

To get a feel for the extent of the literature on depression, consider for a moment Robert Burton's classic exploration of the topic, *The*

Anatomy of Melancholy, first published in 1621 (Burton 1989). Burton, an Oxford fellow, devoted his entire life to exploring the topic of depression, and his book runs for a densely packed 675 pages. Burton covers science, to be sure, but he also explores insights from literature, history, philosophy, and divinity. He finds a wealth of invaluable information on depression, and since Burton's time, additional theories and insights into depression have continued to flourish.

Nowadays, just as in Burton's day, we cannot stop with mainstream scientific approaches lest we blind ourselves to additional insights. In the next chapter, we go beyond mainstream approaches to consider some of the many other contemporary approaches through which depression is understood.

2 What We Also Know

Beyond what appears in mainstream psychiatric science, there are many other things we know about depression. This means that psychiatric science is not simply a summary that distills key information from the vast literature on depression. Textbooks of psychiatry select a particular subset of knowledge on which to focus. But how do textbook writers organize their selection? What choices guide the subset of material they include and exclude? These choices are hardly random. There must be some guiding frame at work. What is this guiding frame?

The most concise answer to this question is that psychiatric textbooks focus largely on material that fits within the *disease model*. To a lesser degree, textbooks also go outside the disease model when they include information from psychotherapy models. But, for the most part, anything outside the disease model is downplayed relative to the attention given to disease model.

What exactly is the "disease model" in psychiatry? What other models beyond the disease model are available? And what do these other models reveal about depression? Once we start considering these questions about the disease model and beyond, a whole host of other theoretical and philosophical questions emerge. What does the fact that there are so many models in psychiatry mean? What are "models" in psychiatry anyway? And how do models function in science and in knowledge making more generally? All of these questions must be taken seriously if we are to understand the vast literature on depression.

This chapter focuses on the first set of questions. We consider the disease model as a "model", we contrast it with several other contemporary models, and we look at what we can learn about depression through these additional models. In Chapter 5, we will return to the deeper theoretical and philosophical issues at stake.

The Disease Model

A good place to begin understanding the "disease model" is with Professor Peter Tyrer (editor of the *British Journal of Psychiatry*) and psychiatrist Derek Steinberg's book *Models for Mental Disorder*. Tyrer and Steinberg explain that the disease model in psychiatry focuses its attention primarily on impaired brain functioning as a consequence of physical and chemical changes. This focus on biological variables gives the disease model a deep affinity with science and medicine. From a disease model perspective, the only real difference between medicine and psychiatry comes from the specificity of the disease. Medicine deals with general malfunctions of the body; psychiatry specializes in malfunctions of the nervous system. As Nobel Prize winning psychiatrist and neuroscientist Eric Kandel put it: "all mental processes, even the most complex psychological processes, derive from operations of the brain. The central tenet of this view is that what we commonly call mind is a range of functions carried out by the brain" (Kandel 1998, 460). Following this logic, disease model advocates argue that since the brain is the organ of the mind, dysfunctions of the mind must therefore be diseases of the brain.

Tyrer and Steinberg (2005, 9) articulate four principles that follow from the psychiatric disease model:

1. Mental pathology is always accompanied by physical pathology.
2. The classification of this pathology allows mental illness to be classified into different disorders that have characteristic features.

3. Mental illness is handicapping and biologically disadvantageous.

4. The cause of mental illness is explicable by its physical consequences.

Following these principles, it makes perfect sense that psychiatrist Nancy Andreason chose to name her best selling introduction to this model *The Broken Brain* (Andreason 1984). The term "broken brain" signifies the diseased, or malfunctioning, brain at the core of mental illness.

Although the term "broken brain" continues to have some purchase, it has gradually been replaced in everyday conversation with the more ubiquitous phrase "chemical imbalance." Since broken brains cannot usually be demonstrated in individual cases, the phrase "chemical imbalance" has also taken over from "the broken brain" as the popular explanatory metaphor of biopsychiatry. The term "chemical imbalance" is more amorphous than "broken brain," but its implication is more or less the same. In a chemical imbalance the brain is still broken, but at the subtle level of chemical functioning rather than at the macro level of brain structures. You may not be able to see it in diagnostic studies, but it is broken nonetheless. Thus, the signifiers "broken brain" and "chemical imbalance" are perfect sound bite translations of the disease model into everyday language.

The options for understanding depression do not stop with the disease model. Moving beyond the disease model, the most common alternative models of depression are the cognitive-behavioral model and the psychoanalytic model. Going a little further from the mainstream, we find family therapy models and humanistic models. And, going even further still we find alternative, spiritual, expressive, and political models of depression. There are also attempts to integrate different approaches. Integrative approaches happen within models and they also happen with models designed specifically for integration, such as the biopsychosocial model. But even if particular models have an integrative dimension, each of these models provides important information about depression that is unique to that particular model.[3] The further we get from the disease model the less we talk in terms of a specific diagnosis of "major depression" and the more broadly in terms of human sadness, suffering, and psychological difference. And the further we get from the disease model, the more depression becomes a subset of these larger human concerns. Yet it is important to include these models because even though they do not always address major depression as outlined in the disease model, they very much address human sadness and misery in its less scientifically delineated forms.

Cognitive-Behavioral Therapy

Compared with the disease model, the cognitive-behavioral model of depression shifts the focus from "broken brains" to "broken thoughts." The focus here is on errors and distortions in thinking that lead to mental illness. Tyrer and Steinberg (2005, 76) describe the model's four central tenants:

1. People's view of their world is determined by their thinking (cognition).
2. Cognition influences symptoms, behavior and attitudes and therefore the main features of mental illness.
3. The persistence of mental illness is a consequence of continuing errors in thinking and maladaptive behaviors that become reinforcing.
4. Significant change in mental disorder is always associated with significant change in cognition and behavior.

Examples of how thoughts lead to feelings include thinking that social situations are threatening and then feeling anxiety, or thinking things are hopeless and then feeling sad. Aaron Beck, the founder of this model, puts it this way, "cognitive theory is based on the assumption that the way individuals interpret their experiences has significant impact on their emotions and actions—indeed, on their overall psychological functioning" (Beck and Newman 2005, 2596).

If a depressed person were to see a cognitive-behavioral therapist, the therapist would look for links between the person's thoughts and their sadness. For the cognitive therapist, depression comes from information processing errors, or "cognitive distortions," that typically include overgeneralization, magnification, and personalization (Beck, Rush, Shaw, and Emery 1979, 14). Depressed people overgeneralize negative thoughts, they magnify their meaning, and they blame themselves for negative events. Cognitive therapists teach depressed patients to monitor their automatic negative thoughts and learn to evaluate these thoughts in a critical but nonjudgmental manner. As clients use the therapy to view their thoughts more objectively, they clarify and modify the meanings assigned to events. Through collaborative effort, the client and the therapist work to produce cognitive shifts that create a "boost in morale" and "improved hopefulness" (Beck and Newman 2005, 2601). Clients are shown how by changing their thoughts they can change their mood, feel better, and cope more effectively.

Psychoanalysis

The psychoanalytic model, often called the "psychodynamic model," is less clearly demarcated than the disease model or cognitive-behaviorism because there are many different schools of psychoanalysis. Psychoanalysis should therefore be seen as a collection of models rather than a single model, depending on which school of psychoanalysis one emphasizes. However, as Tyrer and Steinberg point out, there are clear similarities between various psychoanalytic models and there are basic assumptions common to most psychodynamic therapies (Tyrer and Steinberg 2005, 42).

The basic assumption of psychoanalysis is that problematic patterns of feelings lead to difficulties being in the world. These patterns of feelings are complicated, inconsistent, and often arise from unresolved conflicts in childhood. People fall into a dysfunctional repetition of these feelings because of the ongoing pressure they exert for resolution and because the history of these feelings is often unconscious. As Tyrer and Steinberg put it, "What the patient is aware of, or an attitude he or she adopts, is the tip of the iceberg of feelings, much of which is only partially conscious, or unconscious, but which is influential nonetheless" (2005, 43). Psychodynamic therapists focus their attention on these patterns of unconscious feelings and the way they contribute to the person's current problems. If a person can use the therapeutic situation to gain insight into these feelings and work through the intensity of their original causes, they have a good chance of responding differently to them and avoiding painful repetition.

Of the many models of depression within psychoanalysis the work of George Pollock is particularly helpful. Pollock builds on Sigmund Freud's classic article, "Mourning and Melancholia," to develop a model of depression as pathological mourning. Pollock understands mourning as a necessary adaptation process that allows humans to successfully cope with the losses of life. Death of a loved one, or what Pollock calls bereavement, is just one of the many losses that may elicit a mourning process. The loss of anything that people are attached to can also initiate mourning, whether it be marital separation, divorce, loss of support systems, job loss, serious illness of family members, serious surgical procedures, or ageing, etc.

Once mourning begins, the person can expect to go through a series of phases and stages in which the loss is psychologically metabolized. These stages are often very painful and involve waves of intense emotional desire to be back with the person, place, or thing that has been lost. Being with these painful emotions is what Freud called "the work of mourning." For most people it takes considerable time and emotional support to successfully complete the mourning process, and there is no guarantee that people will come to the other side of mourning. Incomplete mourning or mourning gone awry can leave traces that disturb the person for the rest of his or her lifetime.

Pollock (1978, 273) refers to four possible outcomes of mourning:

1. "normal" or successful resolution which results in "creative activity, creative reinvested living, creative products";
2. "arrestation" of the mourning process with continued denial of the loss and the inability to give up the attachment;
3. "fixations" to earlier developmental stages that are reactivated by incomplete mourning;
4. "pathological" or "deviated" mourning processes that are variously diagnosed by mental health providers as depression or depressive states.

The most successful outcome of mourning "involves not only detachment from internal representations and external absences, but reattachments and freedom (i.e. liberation) at the concluding adaptation" (Pollock 1989, xiii). Pollock refers to this as a process of "mourning-liberation" to emphasize the two mutually related dynamics of mourning—letting go and reattachment.

People suffering from loss may find themselves falling into any of the four alternative outcomes of mourning. The last of these is very similar to what is called "major depression" within the disease model. But rather than focus on broken brains (or broken thoughts as in cognitive-behavioral therapy), Pollock's psychoanalytic model of depression puts human sadness in the context of loss and mourning. By becoming conscious of unresolved mourning and working through these intense feelings in a therapeutic setting, people can overcome the pathological consequences of residual loss, grief, and disappointment. This model, like the one proposed by Horwitz and Wakefield, separates normal from pathological depression. But, unlike Horwitz and Wakefield's model, all depression (pathological or not) begins with loss.

Family Therapy

Like psychoanalysis, family therapy views people's problems in the context of their family interactions. But unlike psychoanalysis, family therapy focuses attention more specifically on current family relations, and it intervenes with the family as a whole. The goal of family therapy is "to identify and change problematic, maladaptive, self-defeating, repetitive relationship patterns" (Goldenberg and Goldenberg 2005, 372). What is also different from psychoanalysis (and most other therapies) is that family therapy conceptualizes the symptomatic family member not as the primary patient but as the "identified patient." The shift from "patient" to "identified patient" marks how family therapy sees the family system itself—not the individual—as the primary unit of treatment. The identified patient may have the most obvious troubles, but they are viewed as a "symptom bearer, expressing the family's disequilibrium or current dysfunction" rather than the source of the problem (p. 372).

Family therapists sometimes compare and contrast the more common individual approaches to their interpersonal approach through a transportation metaphor. If individually oriented therapists are like mechanics, family therapists are like traffic engineers. The mechanic is concerned with "the internal working of vehicles" (Barker 1986, 1), whereas the traffic engineer's job is to "see that vehicles travel smoothly on highways" without bunching up into traffic jams or, worse, wrecking into each other due to poor planning and problematic traffic patterns. From a family therapy perspective, "a well functioning family system helps the development and adjustment of the family members, just as traffic runs more smoothly in a well-designed and efficient road system than in a poor system" (1986, 1). This transportation metaphor helps explain why many family therapists tend to be "present centered" and to "examine here-and-now interactions rather than look to history for antecedent causes" (Becvar and Becvar 2003, 10). From the perspective of a traffic engineer, the road system's history matters less than innovative ways to get traffic flowing again.

Several schools of family therapy have developed over time, but they all have considerable common ground. Irene and Herbert Goldenberg (2005, 386–387) point to several basic premises:

1. People are products of their social connections, and attempts to help them must take family relationships into account.

2. Symptomatic behavior in an individual arises from a context of relationships, and interventions to help that person are most effective when those faulty interactive patterns are altered.

3. Individual symptoms are maintained externally in current family systems transactions.

4. Conjoint sessions in which the family is the therapeutic unit and the focus is on family interaction are more effective in producing change than attempts to uncover intrapsychic problems in individuals by therapy via individual sessions.

5. Assessing family subsystems and the permeability of boundaries within the family and between the family and the outside world offers important clues regarding family organization and susceptibility to change.

6. Traditional psychiatric diagnostic labels based on individual psychopathology fail to provide an understanding of family dysfunctions and tend to pathologize individuals.

7. The goal of family therapy is to change maladaptive or dysfunctional family interactive patterns.

All of these common features focus on a family systems frame of reference. They see the family as a "complexly organized, durable, causal network of related parts that together constitute an entity larger than the simple sum of its individual members" (Goldenberg and Goldenberg 2005, 373).

If a person suffering from depression were to see a family therapist, the therapist would listen to their story from this interactive perspective. The therapist would make connections between the person's symptoms and their family situation, and the therapist would see the person as the identified patient but not as the source of the problems. Instead, the therapist would understand the locus of difficulty to be at the level of the family itself and would see vulnerabilities in the family that likely contributed to this difficulty. Based on this assessment, the family therapist would help the family reframe the depressed person's problem so that they better understood the person's symptoms as emerging from larger family relations. The therapist would help them see that treating the depressed person alone would likely result in a return of symptoms if the family context were not addressed. Through the course of family work both the person with depression and the family would develop "more effective coping skills and learn better ways to ask for what they want from one another" (Goldenberg and Goldenberg 2005, 399).

Humanistic Psychotherapy

Humanistic psychotherapy emphasizes four central themes:

1. a phenomenological approach that views the client as the expert of his or her own experience;
2. a deep commitment to human capacities for self-growth and actualization;
3. a belief in the human agency as the final arbitrator of choice and self-determination;
4. a person-centered focus that gives a deep respect for the uniqueness of each individual.

                           (Rice and Greenberg 1992, 198–199)

Different humanistic therapies work with these themes in different ways. Of the three leading alternatives—person-centered, gestalt, and existential—the most influential (at least in the U.S.) is Carl Rogers's person-centered approach.

Rogers began his psychotherapeutic work by applying a traditional diagnostic, prescriptive, and professionally impersonal stance. But his experience with clients left him so disenchanted with this approach that he switched tactics. Indeed, he practically reversed his previous stance. He "tried listening and following the clients' lead rather than assuming the role of the expert" (Raskin and Rogers 2005, 135). Over time, he drew on an existentialist and phenomenological analysis to develop a form of therapy that put understanding the person's subjective experience at the heart of the therapeutic enterprise. Rogers aimed to mirror the client's phenomenology as faithfully as possible, without disagreeing, contradicting, or giving outside insight from the therapist perspective.

The goal was to create an unalienating environment of understanding from which the person could develop their own solutions and stimulate their inborn capacity for growth and development. The open and candid self-exploration Rogers aimed for could only be achieved in the context of a close and trusting relationship. Rogers carefully articulated what he came to see as the three most essential ingredients of this kind of helping relationship: congruence, empathy, and positive regard.

Congruence refers to the therapist's ability to be present and transparent to the client. The therapist works with the client without facade and does not pretend to be something they do not feel. Within the boundaries of the therapeutic relationship, the therapist therefore provides the client with a genuine relationship rather than what could be called a "pseudo-relationship" that gives in to the temptation to hide behind a mask of professionalism. *Empathy* focuses on the importance of understanding the client's perspective from within the client's frame of reference. As Rogers puts it, empathy is "an active experiencing with the client of the feelings to which [the client] gives expression," (Raskin and Rogers 2005, 145). *Positive regard* is the third essential ingredient for person-centered therapy. Other terms that have been used for this ingredient are warmth, acceptance, non-possessive caring, and prizing. Rogers refers to positive regard as a "kind of love," comparing the notion of "love" to the theologian's term *agape*, which "respects the other person as a separate individual and does not possess him. It is a kind of liking which has strength, and which is not demanding" (quoted in Shaffer 1978, 84).

Central to Rogers and other humanistic psychologists is the metaphor of a person as an "organismic self." In stark contrast to the mechanistic models of self found in biopsychiatry or cognitive-behavioral approaches, this organismic self is present at birth, has inherent strivings of its own, and most importantly has an inborn capacity for self-repair and self-actualization (Shaffer 1978, 81). Rogers found that the three therapeutic ingredients allowed this inborn capacity, or organismic self, to regenerate. When the therapeutic conditions were met—when Rogers was able to be real, to be empathically in tune, and to be deeply accepting—the people he worked with rediscovered a capacity for growth. These conditions were the soil, the sunlight, and the moisture needed for healthy growth and regeneration. When people were supplied with these conditions, they were able to work out within themselves an understanding of the aspects of their life causing pain or dissatisfaction. They reorganized their personality and their relationships with life in ways that were more rewarding and fulfilling. Plus, they came to value themselves more highly, were more confident and self directing, and were more open to experience and more accepting of others. Rogers argued that:

> whether one calls it a growth tendency, a drive toward self-actualization, or a forward-moving directional tendency, it is the mainspring of life, and is, in the last analysis, the tendency upon which all psychotherapy depends. It is the urge which is evident in all organic and human life—to expand, extend, become autonomous, develop, and mature.
>
> (Rogers 1961, 35)

For Rogers, the task of therapy was to revitalize the person's natural healing capacity. People's tendency toward growth:

> may become deeply buried under layer after layer of incrusted psychological defenses; it may be hidden behind elaborate facades which deny its existence; but it is my belief that it exists in every individual, and awaits only the proper conditions to be released and expressed.
>
> (Rogers 1961, 35)

With this background in mind, what would a person-centered therapy look like for a person with depression? Person-centered therapy is similar to other therapies in that the therapist would be available for individual meetings to help the person work through their difficulties. The difference would be in the therapist style. Rather than approach the client as an "expert" who "knows" the causes of their mental suffering (as would happen in the disease model, cognitive therapy, or psychoanalysis), a person-centered therapist would work toward creating a therapeutic relationship in which the client could develop their own understandings and resolutions to their troubles. The humanistic therapist would work to reinvigorate the person's natural healing capacity rather than try to fix "broken brains" or "cognitive distortions."

Alternative Models

A myriad of "alternative" models on depression exist—far too many, in fact, to review in detail. But two options that are particularly insightful for depression come from holistic healers who use yoga and those who use meditation in the care of sadness. Yoga techniques for depression are worked out by Amy Weintraub in her book *Yoga for Depression*. Weintraub first became interested in depression through her own experiences. She was treated with mainstream psychotherapy and medication with little response; so she turned to Yoga for help. Within a year of Yoga practice, she felt much better and was no longer taking medication. She was so impressed with the power of Yoga breathing and posture techniques along with the wisdom of the yogi tradition, she decided to become a certified Yoga teacher.

Weintraub uses Kripalu Yoga practices, which provide a systematic method for maintaining physical and emotional health. Kripalu Yoga teaches that sadness and suffering come when we are too tightly bound to current reality and therefore cut off from the greater cosmos. "As we live farther and farther from the truth of our wholeness, we become ignorant of that wholeness and live as though we are separate and alone" (Weintraub 2004, 13). Yoga practice provides an opportunity to wake up from ignorance, "to transcend our identification with our bodies, our clinging to what we love, our avoidance of what we hate, our fear of death" (2004, 13). Ultimately, practicing yoga leads to a "healing state, a blissful feeling wherein you may lose the sense of yourself as a being separate from the universe and gain a momentary sense of union" (2004, 12).

A somewhat similar alternative for depression evolves from the traditions of Zen meditation. Philip Martin's book *The Zen Path Through Depression* provides a good example. Like Weintraub, Martin turned to alternative therapeutic practice as a result of his own experiences. At the age of thirty-seven, he went through a devastating depression despite the fact that he had been practicing Zen Buddhism for many years. At first, he approached his sadness from a mainstream perspective and saw it as a "disease" completely separate from his spirituality. After all, it seemed that depression stole all he found life-giving, including his spiritual practice. But separating his depression from his spirituality turned out to be a passing phase.

With time and continued devotion Martin found a way to connect his sadness and despair to his Zen practices. Ultimately, he discovered that the downward movement of depression allowed him to settle more fully into his spiritual life and provided an opportunity for spiritual opening and learning. Depression, Martin concluded:

> is not just of the body and mind, but also of the heart. Depression offers us an opportunity to deepen our sprit, our lives, and our hearts. There is much that we can learn about ourselves and our world through this journey. Through attentive compassionate practice with depression, it is possible to experience an even deeper healing, and grow in our spiritual lives.
> (Martin 1999, xii)

Martin went on to become a psychiatric social worker, and his book provides a guide to the wilderness of depression through a series of meditative practices. Martin shows his readers how to sit in a quiet place either in a lotus position or on a cushion or chair with their hands folded in their lap and their gaze dropped a few feet in front of them. Once comfortable, Martin suggests the following:

· Feel the rising and falling in your of your belly as you breathe in and out. If you wish, you may think "in" and "out" with your breathing.

Become aware of the space around you. Feel that this is your space, your ground, your home. You are like a pebble sinking down through a river to settle on the bottom, where the waves and currents can't touch you. Envision yourself sitting on a throne, or a mountaintop—anywhere that seems a powerful place to you. Say three times to yourself, "this is where I make my stand." You are immoveable here. You are strong and safe in this spot. All fears, all grief, all pain can come and wash over and through you, and not wash you away.

Now come back again to your breath, following it in and out, as your belly rises and falls. Your breath is the anchor that is always there, that will hold you in this place. Become aware that this place where you sit is immense and extends into all directions. It is large enough to contain whatever you choose to invite in. Welcome your feelings of fear, your pain, your depression into this place. Tell the depression that it need not feel excluded from this place, that in this place it will receive understanding and compassion. Invite into this place as well any deities, energies, that you wish. Especially those that give you strength—but also, if you would like those that may bring your fear. Again come back to your breath, and feel the immensity of the place within which you sit like a mountain.

When you are ready to return, remind all those you have invited in that they are welcome to return again when you come back. Remind yourself that this place waits for you, at any time you wish it. Sit, enjoying this place your have created. Let your attention rise through your chest, shoulders, and neck, and slowly open your eyes.

(Martin 1999, 5)

Martin gives guided meditations like this for many of the most difficult aspects of depression: pain, fear, doubt, anger, suffering, loneliness, death, desire, impermanence, etc. He shows how to ease these feelings through meditations and how doing so may enrich the soul while it mends the spirit. Stopping and listening to depression through meditative practices calls the meditator to the most profound questions of living: Why are we born? Why must we suffer and die? Who are we? How shall we live in this moment? These questions, along with the pain and suffering that accompanies them, are the seeds of freedom. Painful and frightening as this approach to depression may be, the rewards can be immense. When the sufferer of depression takes a stand and does not run, he or she learns what depression has to teach. "To do so is not to give in to depression, but rather to take the first step in healing our pain and suffering" (Martin 1999, 3).

Cheri Huber, a teacher of Zen meditation, takes a similar approach to depression, but she goes one step further. Although Martin teaches how it is possible to welcome depression into one's meditative space, he does so with the intent of changing or working through the depression. This idea—the idea that depression should be changed— is an idea that runs through all the approaches we have reviewed so far. For Huber, by contrast, the idea that one must change depression can be one of depression's most painful dimensions. Rather than try to change their sad and painful feelings, Huber suggests that Zen meditative practices allow people with depression to accept themselves at a deeper level and to embrace themselves with love and compassion. This embrace does not happen after the depression passes, but "RIGHT NOW!" (Huber 1999, 1). If you are depressed you should be depressed:

> This moment is the only moment you have. HAVE IT! Don't be afraid to experience your experience. There is nothing to fear . . . Nothing awful is going on except the way [you] feel, and if [you] didn't hate the feeling, it wouldn't be awful.
>
> (Huber 1999, 107–108)

How we treat our self in depression, in other words, may be more important than getting over depression. "Hating or rejecting this moment is not good practice for loving and accepting myself in another" (1999, 108). Huber therefore uses meditative practices to help people to feel what they feel and think what they think. "Whatever you are doing, love yourself for doing it. Whatever you are thinking, love yourself for thinking it" (1999, 133). And, most important, even if you do not like the feelings of sadness or despair, "love yourself for not liking it" (1999, 133).

Religious Approaches

A common frame for understanding the relationship between religious life and depression is the notion of a "dark night of the soul" (Moore 2004). For example, in Christian churches, pastoral counselors often meet people who are going through periods of intense psychic pain with feelings of emptiness, meaninglessness, loneliness, sadness and despair. These intense states, or "dark nights" as they are often called, tend to occur in two periods of a devotee's life: 1) during incubation periods just before a spiritual breakthrough into a new, different, and ultimately higher level of spiritual practice or awareness; or 2) during times when a devotee has gotten too far away from his or her religious practice.

The first of these "dark nights" resembles what William James famously called the "twice-born." For James, the heart of religious experience comes precisely from its capacity to transform melancholy feelings of meaninglessness, ominous evil, and deep personal guilt. Religion, for James, is explicitly understandable as an invaluable response to these most dire of human states. When people go through a religious conversion, they break through to the other side of these dark feelings. They become "twice-born," and they achieve a state of assurance and salvation. Meaningfulness emerges, there is a triumph of ultimate goodness, the world becomes more beautiful and real, and there is a "loss of all worry" with a "sense that all is intimately well with one." The twice-born have feelings of peace, harmony, and a *"willingness to be*, even though the outer conditions remain the same" (James 1982, 248). In addition, the twice born are empowered to the point that previous inhibitions and conflicts often melt away (Taylor 2002, 37). James calls this alternative psychic state "saint-liness," which brings the direct feeling of a greater power and a corresponding sense of elation and freedom. In saintliness, "the outlines of confining selfhood melt down" and there is a "shifting of the emotional center towards loving and harmonious affections" (James 1982, 271–273).

The second form of "dark night" is similar except that it occurs not at a moment of spiritual breakthrough, but at times when a person gets too distant from his or her religious roots. For this form of dark night, pastoral counselor Agenta Schreurs uses the evocative phrase "spirituality in exile" (Schreurs 2002, 45). The phrase refers to a spiritual practitioner who has wandered, or who has been forced, too far from their religious homeland: someone who has lost their sense of belonging and is left isolated and alone. Schreurs finds that spirituality in exile is particularly common in contemporary Western cultures because the lure of a material and secular life distracts people from their religious practice. The religious devotee who has lost touch with their religion often goes through the melancholic pain of spiritual exile that includes all the painful emotions James describes. These feelings are not a sign of pathology for religious practitioners but a potent signal that guides the devotee back to the fold of religious faith and tradition.

Expressive Therapy and Creativity

Expressive therapy models parallel the creative process, and, as such, expressive therapy draws out similar features between the therapeutic work and creative expression. For the expressive therapist, the artist and the person in therapy have in common the need to explore their internal psychic life and their relations to the surrounding world. Both the artist and the person in therapy use this awareness to transform their experiences through self expression. Expressive therapists focus their attention along a continuum that places more or less emphasis on the therapy side or on the artist side, where one side of the continuum may be called "art *in* therapy" and the other side may be called "art *as* therapy" (Edwards 2004, 1). The distinction sounds subtle, but the lived experience between these two approaches can be tremendous.

The expressive therapist working from the art *in* therapy side of the continuum uses artistic expression to help the person access psychic materials that can then be processed through a therapeutic relationship. Art *in* therapy therefore functions similar to the way Freud used free association and dream analysis. For a person with depression using an art *in* therapy model, artistic expression helps the person and the therapist tune into aspects of the person's thoughts, feelings, and perceptions that are difficult for the person to reach through direct conversation alone. Once this material becomes available through art, expressive therapists help the person process the depressive material and work it through in ways similar to other therapists.

At the other end of the continuum, when the focus is on art *as* therapy, the expressive therapist focuses less on standard therapeutic goals and more on helping people achieve creative expression. This side of the continuum makes sense because art alone, independent of traditionally defined therapeutic goals, can be tremendously healing for depression. First, many people find art to be deeply engaging. When a person is absorbed in the process of art, other aspects of life, even painful depressive aspects, may drift into the background. Furthermore, art allows people to take hard-to-reach experiences of depression and share them with an audience. These experiences, which might otherwise be toxic or alienating, find a voice through creative expression so that the artist is no longer isolated and alone with them.

In addition, art rewards people for their sensitivity to the suffering of the world. To be an artist, one must be able to pick up on aspects of inner life and the world that often escape other people. This sensitivity, which is often coded negatively in the context of most approaches to depression (most therapeutic approaches suggest that people "stop being so sensitive"), is coded positively in the context of creative expression. A highly sensitive "patient" may be a bad thing, but a highly sensitive "artist" is nearly always a good thing. Finally, art takes depressive experiences that may otherwise be seen as ugly or sad and turns them into something aesthetically beautiful and/or politically moving. Art therefore brings the artist outside of their own pre-occupations and into the community. It gives people an invaluable role in making the world a better place.

Expressive therapists vary in how much they emphasize art *in* therapy compared with art *as* therapy. Some primarily focus on the former, some on the latter. Most focus on a combination. It is important to note, however, that the further we move toward the art *as* therapy side the more the therapeutic language recedes and the creative language emerges. If one goes far enough down this continuum, artistic work easily escapes the context of expressive therapy altogether and becomes simply art. In other words, one does not need to be in expressive therapy to do artistic work. One may simply become an artist. The practical implications of becoming an artist will mean not going to a therapist at all but rather taking art classes, setting up a studio, joining an artistic community, etc. The ideas and language of "therapy" may be the farthest thing from the artist's mind.

Social and Political Approaches

Social and political approaches to depression utilize a social model that moves beyond individual variables to consider the larger social-cultural context of the individual's situation. Social models are similar to family models in this way, except that social models consider cultural and political dynamics outside the scope of the family. Tyrer and Steinberg (2005, 100) point to four basic tenets of the social model:

1. Difficulties are often triggered by life events outside the individual.
2. Social and cultural forces linked to status and role often precipitate difficulties.
3. Mental disorders often become and remain "disordered" because of societal influences.
4. Much apparent mental disorder has been falsely labeled and should be regarded as a temporary maladjustment.

Feminist therapy approaches have developed this model in detail and their work centers on a key insight for all of feminist work: *the personal is political.* Carol Hanisch first coined this phrase in the early years of second wave feminism when she noted how feminist political discussions tended to get mired in debates over personal verses political priorities (Humm 1992, 1). Hanisch's experience in early consciousness raising groups made it clear that these debates rested on a false binary: "One of the first things we discover in these groups is that personal problems are political problems." Hanisch found that intimate personal conversations with other women gave her:

> [a] political understanding which all my reading, all my "political discussions," all my "political action," all my four-odd years in the movement never gave me. I've been forced to take off the rose-colored glasses and face the awful truth about how grim my life really is as a woman.
>
> (Hanisch 1971, 152–153)

Hanisch argued persuasively that the two issues—personal and political —are very much intertwined, and her phrase "the personal is political" became a rallying cry not only for feminist psychotherapy but for second wave feminism more broadly.

From a social and political perspective, feminist therapists see many of the symptoms of depression not as individual pathology but as the consequences of oppression and signs of subsequent internalized oppression. Dana Crowley Jack provides a good example of this approach in her book *Silencing the Self: Women and Depression*. Early in her career Jack was struck with the fact that the rates of depression are twice as high for women as for men, and she set herself the task of understanding what it is about "women's inner and outer worlds that creates this vulnerability to the hopelessness and pain of depression" (Jack 1991, 2). She found herself deeply dissatisfied with mainstream approaches that failed to address gender. The major concepts used in these approaches too often organize people's problems through patriarchal norms of independence and self-sufficiency. As a result, feminine/ maternal preferences for relationships and emotional intimacy come to be pathologized as neurotic and dependent. "A woman is caught in a double bind: society still pushes her to define herself through [feminine/maternal] relationships, but then it invalidates her wish for connection by derogating the importance of attachments" (1991, 6).

When Jack considered women's vulnerability for depression through this perspective, she found that feminine/maternal women often complained of "losing themselves" in relationships with masculine partners. One of her clients, Susan, put it this way:

> I like closeness. I like companionship. I like somebody, an intimate closeness, even with a best friend. I was always so close to my mother . . . I was used to that all through my childhood, having an intimate closeness . . . someone that shared my feelings, my fears, my doubts, my happiness, my achievements, my failures. And I've never had that with my husband. I can't talk to him on those levels . . . He lives in a very concrete, day-to-day, black-and-white world.
>
> (Jack 1991, 4)

Susan, like many others, came to see her needs for closeness as a sign of dependence and weakness. She had the feeling that her "need for intimacy" and "deep level of friendship or relationships with people was sort of bad," and she began to believe "there was something the matter" with her (1991, 5).

Jack observes that Susan uses the language of patriarchy to deny what, on another level, she values and desires. The patriarchal power dynamics of her relationship with her husband forces her to stifle these desires:

> Susan cannot ask for what she wants most—an intimate closeness. Hidden from her description is the reason why she cannot ask: inequality mutes her ability to communicate directly about her needs. She does not feel entitled to as to have her needs filled, nor does she feel they are legitimate.
>
> (Jack 1991, 5)

Susan is forced to bury part of her self to relate to her husband, and over time this self-silencing combined with a sense of inferiority leads to feelings of despair, hopelessness, and worthlessness. From Jack's perspective, these depressed feelings arise not from individual pathology; instead they are the expectable outcome of oppressive environments and the internalization of oppressive values.

For women of color, the gender dynamic Jack describes is often further complicated by ethnopolitical issues as well. Lillian Comas-Diaz points out that women of color exposed to dominant Western White cultures often experience what could be called "cultural Stockholm syndrome" or "post-colonization stress" disorder (Comas-Diaz 2000, 1320). Racism and cultural imperialism imposes dominant values as inevitable and superior, leading minority groups to accept not only dominant cultural values but also the prevailing negative stereotypes of their own group. This internalized colonization can create pervasive feelings of identity conflict, alienation, and self-denial that can further lead to psychological effects of shame, rage, and depression:

> Consequently, the experiences of racism, sexism, identity, conflict, oppression, cultural adaptation, environmental stressors,

plus internalized colonization prevalent amount and specific to many women of color, constitute critical considerations in the delivery of relevant psychotherapeutic services.

(Comas-Diaz 1994, 288)

Social models were also prominent among a group of theorists and therapists who became collectively labeled "anti-psychiatry." Authors in this group, such as Erving Goffman (1961), R. D. Laing (1967), Thomas Scheff (1966), and Thomas Szasz (1961), differed widely in their philosophies but their main tenet was clear. "Mental illness," like depression, is not an objective medical reality. Instead, what we call mental illness is either a negative label enforced for social control or a political strategy for coping in a mad world. As Laing put it, "the apparent irrationality of the single 'psychotic' individual" may often be understood "within the context of the family." And the irrationality of the family can be understood if it is placed "within the context of yet larger organizations and institutions" (Laing 1968, 15). Put in social context in this way, psychic pain such as depression has a political legitimacy of its own that is often erased by models of psychic difference that emphasize pathology and internal causes (Mirowsky and Ross 2003). Rather than an internal pathology, mental difference and depression can be the beginning of a personal and social resistance or of a healing process and should not be suppressed through therapeutic interventions.

Consumer activism in psychiatry has picked up on these themes and has used a social model to show how psychiatry itself can be a source of suffering (Lewis 2006b). A consumer activist group called the Icarus Project provides a good example. The Icarus Project was started in 2002 by Sascha DuBrul and Ashley McNamara—two young psychiatric service users who were diagnosed with "Bipolar Disorder" in their twenties and found themselves struggling as much with the standards of psychiatric care as with their own emotional intensities. Although the initial focus was bipolar disorder, the Icarus Project has extended its focus to an array of psychiatric diagnoses including depression.

For DuBrul and McNamara, the core of the problem with psychiatry was that it overemphasized scientific ideals of "disease" and "cure."

DuBrul and McNamara were both told by their psychiatrists that bipolar disorder was a disease that needed to be treated and, if possible, cured. They did not dismiss psychiatry and psychiatric treatments, but they felt this approach missed something crucial. They agreed that their psychic differences could cause them tremendous difficulties, but they also found it a mistake to emphasize a language of pathology and broken brains. For DuBrul and McNamara, the psychic differences that most led to their diagnosis—their intense passions—were not simply a "disease," because these passions were also part of who they were as people. These passions were part of what they, and others, found most creative, exceptional, and valuable about them.

Instead of accepting or rejecting the prevailing standards of psychiatric care, DuBrul and McNamara set out to create a grassroots alternative community for healing and recovery. As McNamara explains:

> We began The Icarus Project as a way of creating space for people to share their trajectories through this under-charted world of blackness and brilliance and the million shades of gray that the medical establishment has no idea how to describe.
>
> (Horrigan 2005)

Using their artistic skills and their often manic energy, they created a website that is the hub of the project (http://theicarusproject.net/). This website is designed to be an electronic oasis for people struggling with psychic difference of all sorts and who find that they do not fit well with the mainstream. It is meant to be place to let loose, to share hopes and fears and stories, and to benefit from the community and wisdom of people who understand and have often been there before. After the initial website was set up, the project grew in members and went on to create its own publications, such as *Navigating the Space Between Brilliance and Madness* and *Friends Make the Best Medicine: A Guide to Creating Community Mental Health Support Networks*. These resources have allowed The Icarus Project to move from a virtual community to a material community of mutual support in several cities around the country.

Throughout this process, Icarus Project members have been led by a moving mission statement first penned by DuBrul and McNamara in the early days of their work. The statement begins:

> Defining ourselves outside convention we see our condition as a dangerous gift to be cultivated and taken care of rather than [simply] a disease or disorder needing to be "cured." With this double edged blessing we have the ability to fly to places of great vision and creativity, but like the boy Icarus, we also have the potential to fly dangerously close to the sun—into realms of delusion and psychosis—and crash in a blaze of fire and confusion. At our heights we may find ourselves capable of creating music, art, words, and inventions which touch people's souls and change the course of history.
>
> (Icarus Project 2004)

DuBrul and McNamara's statement goes on to acknowledge the risks they bear in defining their situations outside convention and the possible perils of seeing their madness as dangerous gifts. They accept that their psychic differences could leave them "alienated and alone, incarcerated in psychiatric institutions" or at worst "dead by our own hands." However, in spite of these very real dangers, they also recognize the importance of acknowledging how madness and creativity are deeply intertwined and how, in fact, madness and creativity can be "tools of inspiration and hope in this repressed and damaged society." As they put it, "We understand that we are members of a group that has been misunderstood and persecuted throughout history, but has also been responsible for some of its most brilliant creations. And we are proud" (Icarus Project 2004).

Bringing these strands of the Icarus Project together, we can see that this approach creates an integrated model that blends pathological models with creative and political models. The goal is to recognize the dangers and pitfalls of madness and to celebrate and tap into the "true potential that lies between brilliance and madness." While putting in the necessary effort to stay balanced and grounded and to lead full and independent lives (which might include psychiatric medications

and/or psychotherapy), the Icarus Project aims to separate madness
"from the reductionist framework offered by the current mental
health establishment" and, in doing so, make the world a "better, more
beautiful, and way more interesting" place. The goal, according to
DuBrul and McNamara's statement, is "not just to survive, but to
thrive," and they will do this by learning "from each others' mistakes
and victories, stories and art, and create a new culture and language
that resonates with our actual experiences of 'disorder'" (Icarus Project
2004).

Biopsychosocial Model

There have also been a variety of clinical attempts to integrate different
models. The most widely used version is George Engel's Biopsychosocial Model (Engel 1977, 1980). Engel stood on the shoulders of Von
Bertalanffy's systems theory of biology to organize the many approaches
to psychiatry into three broad groups: biological, psychological, and
social. For Engel, if we are to understand people, we must bring
together all three groups.

When Engel applied his biopsychosocial model to problems such as
depression, he argued that in any clinical situation the three separate
systems (the biological, the personal, and the social) must be simultaneously considered (Engel 1980). If there is room for improvement
in any of these systems, the clinician and patient work together toward
that end. For example, improvement might be available in the social
system through an alternative living situation or job, in the personal
system through alternative subjective meaning structures, and in the
biological system through the biomedical interventions. The clinician
keeps all three systems in mind simultaneously. Any improvement in
one system is assumed to result in some improvement for the other
systems as well. Engel keeps open which system "causes" the depression,
since all systems can affect each other. In any particular case, one system
may be more responsible than another, but still the clinician should
keep a focus on all three.

It may be tempting to see integrative models such as the
biopsychosocial model or the Icarus Project as the solution to multiple
models since these integrative models consider a variety of variables
and perspectives. But things are not so simple. The biopsychosocial

model, for example, is still a model, and it too organizes clinical interpretations of depression in a particular way. Beyond this, the biopsychosocial model does little if anything with the creative, political, or spiritual models of depression. Nor does it say anything about competing models within a single dimension—such as the alternatives between psychoanalysis and cognitive-behavioral at the psychological level or the alternatives between family and political at the social level.

Rather than seeing the biopsychosocial model or the Icarus project as the solution to multiple models of depression, it seems better to see these approaches as possibilities in a long line of model options. This certainly does not make the biopsychosocial model or the Icarus Project inferior to other models, but it also does not make them superior. Like all models, these approaches include some things, but leave out others; they can often be helpful, but they can also have limitations.

Conclusion

Each of these contemporary models of depression provides invaluable insight. Each gives us ways to makes sense of depression and each provides solutions for coping. In our time, the disease model is the most widespread of the group. It receives the most attention and the most research funding. It draws our brightest and most ingenious thinkers. This attention to the disease model can make it seem much more important and compelling than the other models. It makes it seem as if the other models will soon fade away and the disease model will be all we need to understand depression.

But when we turn from a contemporary overview to the historical record, we get a deeper sense of how persistent multiple models have been across time. We see how, at different times, other models have been at the attention of our brightest and the most brilliant thinkers. And, most important, we get a deeper sense of the continued viability of these models and how unlikely it is that one model will capture the flag for very long. Depression is too open to diverse approaches for a single model to dominate in the long run. Thus, for a deeper understanding of the models, it helps to leave the contemporary literature and turn to history.

PART II
HISTORICAL AND CULTURAL PERSPECTIVES

3 Western History

A historical perspective on depression reinforces our appreciation of multiple models of depression. From a historical perspective, multiple models of depression are nothing new. Western culture has approached depression from a variety of perspectives over time, and these diverse approaches provide the antecedents of today's models of depression. History shows us the brilliance that has gone into the models and how persistent a multiplicity of approaches to depression has been over time. To understand this history, we will start with representations of depression from the ancient world. From there, we move to classical Greece, the Middle Ages, the Renaissance, the Enlightenment, the Romantic age, and modern times. Clearly this will be a quick sampling tour, which cannot do justice to the many subtleties involved. Nonetheless, it is essential to have a historical perspective on today's models of depression, which have evolved from what has come before and are a transient prelude to future possibilities.

Throughout this history of depression, I focus on melancholic subjectivity and intense sadness, keeping the signifiers "depression," "melancholy," and "melancholia" open-ended, without drawing sharp distinctions between them. From the outset I also do not separate distinctions such as "mild versus severe," "normal versus pathological," "personality verses disease," or "mourning verses melancholia." It is true that different approaches to depression differentiate different kinds of depression. But to adopt a differential scheme in advance means to adopt a particular approach to depression. Our goal here is to understand different approaches to depression from within their own systems of thought.

Ancient World

The oldest known depiction of intense sadness and depression goes back to the third millennium BC and the *Epic of Gilgamesh*. One thousand years older than the *Iliad* or the Bible, *Gilgamesh* is based on a historical king who reigned in Mesopotamia around 2750 BC. The epic tells the story of Gilgamesh and his deep friendship with Enkidu. Before meeting Enkidu, Gilgamesh had been a restless, bored, and despotic king. But with Enkidu, he finds a companion who helps him settle and find purpose. Both men are larger than life, stronger and more powerful than all of their peers. They form a seemingly invincible team, and together they travel the world in search of heroic adventure, battle, and tests of strength. These battles are often caught up in self-aggrandizement and many are ill advised, but nevertheless when Gilgamesh and Enkidu are together Gilgamesh is content and happy with his life.

The two friends' battles eventually anger the gods to the point that Enkidu is punished with death. When Gilgamesh learns of Enkidu's death, he falls into the depths of despair and his sorrowful lament echoes through the ages:

> My beloved friend is dead, he is dead.
> My beloved brother is dead. I will mourn
> as long as I breathe. I will sob for him
> like a woman who has lost her only child.
>
> (Mitchell 2004, 44)

Gilgamesh's grief was so intense that:

> he paced in front of [Enkidu], back and forth,
> like a lioness whose cubs are trapped in a pit,

he tore out clumps of his hair, tore off
his magnificent robes as though they were cursed

(p. 45)

His sorrow does not resolve easily, and long after Enkidu has died, Gilgamesh continues to suffer. The sadness over Enkidu stirs up other sadnesses within him—particularly the woe of his own mortality. "Must I die too? Must I be as lifeless as Enkidu? How can I bear this sorrow that gnaws at my belly this fear of death, that restlessly drives me onward?" (p. 159). These combined sadnesses make it impossible for Gilgamesh to let go of his sorrow, and they send him on a desperate quest for immortality. No matter how valiantly he searches, however, the quest for immortality turns out to be futile. Gilgamesh is left with nothing to do but to return home.

The *Epic of Gilgamesh* is instructive in that it shows an approach to intense sadness and despair tied to external events and the consequence of powerful forces—natural and supernatural. Gilgamesh's sadness does not come from nowhere; it is caused by calamity and corresponding desolation. This model goes forward throughout ancient times. Job, the Bible's great melancholic, suffers because of his tremendous misfortune (Greenberg 2010, 25–38). In the *Iliad*, Bellerophon suffers a mad melancholy after he is punished by the gods for his hubris. And Achilles suffers tremendous despair after the death of his beloved friend, Patroclus:

> A black cloud of grief swallowed up Achilles. With both hands he scooped up soot and dust and poured it on his head, covering his handsome face with dirt, covering his sweet-smelling tunic with black ash. He lay sprawling—his mighty warrior's massive body collapsed and stretched out in the dust. With his hands, he tugged at his own hair, disfiguring himself.
>
> (Homer 2006, 397)

In each of these ancient tales, the story of intense sorrow is also a story of hardship and adversity. The model is clear. People feel bad when bad things happen to them. Whether the bad things are caused by fate, bad luck, or the gods, the person's sadness is perfectly understandable.

The solution is clear as well—change the external circumstances causing the bad feelings. Gilgamesh cannot bring Enkidu back to life, but he can attempt to change the circumstance of human mortality. He does not succeed, but the approach he takes follows logically from his model of depression.

Echoes of this model are very much with us today. We too feel that if people suffer from misfortunes of fate or bad luck (if bad things happen to us), then this yields understandable suffering and despair. For secular contemporaries, a commonly described external force is social oppression (such as sexism, racism, or classism)—or, as we saw in the last chapter, "the personal is political." For these contemporaries, the model is similar to ancient times—external hardship can cause human misery. The solution is similar as well—if we really care about depression, we must change the social order to reduce human oppression.

Classical Greece

Moving forward in time, the three approaches to depression we highlight from classical Greece are those seen in Greek tragedy, medical theory, and philosophy. All three shift the focus of depression from external sources to internal sources. But they do so in very different ways.

The Greek tragedies, as a group, revolve around conflict and dramatic tension. Some of this conflict is external, such as conflict between man and gods or between man and man, but much of it involves internal, or psychological, conflict: "between one ideal of honor and another, between one part of the hero and another, between one part of the self and another" (Simon 1978, 90). Consider Sophocles' play Ajax from the fifth century BC. Ajax, the most well-known depressive in Greek tragedy, suffers from a conflict between his ideals of himself as a warrior and his sense of failure and humiliation. Sophocles depicts Ajax as driven into deep despair from this conflict: "he wailed and he wailed in anguish . . . [and] when he groaned it was no shrill lament but deep like the bellow of a bull" (Sophocles 1999, 38, lines 345–350). Ajax's depression is so bad he refuses to eat or drink, and he develops a suicidal plan to bury his sword in the ground and thrust himself upon it. Ajax gets little relief from this plan because even his suicidal intent is in deep conflict with his desire to live so he can take care of his wife and child. Eventually, however, his suicidal intent wins out and Ajax kills himself with his own sword.

In this example, the causes of Ajax's despair are not all internal. The external causes include misfortunes similar those of Gilgamesh. Before Ajax's depression, he was denied rewards that he thought he deserved and he was tricked by the gods into much of his humiliation. But, in addition to these external causes, a major part of Ajax's despair involves internal psychological conflict, and this notion of internal psychological conflict at the root of human despair introduces a new perspective on depression. Aspects of this model go forward in Western history all the way to Freud and his psychoanalytic model of unconscious conflict and unresolved feelings at the root of depression (Simon 1978, 277).

Greek medical writings on melancholia maintain this internal focus, but they do so through a new set of internal variables. Starting with Hippocrates (approx 400 BC), classical physicians link the symptoms of depression with physical disease and biological causes. These Hippocratic writings do not completely deny misfortune, supernatural causes, or psychological conflict, but the model of depression developed in Greek medical writings sees these factors as largely beyond the reach of medicine and medical explanation (Drabkin 1955, 224).

The medical logic of depression from this time develops from a humoral theory of the body. Classical Greek science held that there were four elements: earth, air, fire, and water. Each element had its own quality: fire associated with heat, air with cold, water with moisture, and earth with dryness. The four bodily humors—blood, yellow bile, phlegm, and black bile—were related to the four elements, the qualities of these elements, and also the four seasons (Jackson 1986, 7):

Humor	Qualities	Season
Blood	Warm and moist	Spring
Yellow bile	Warm and dry	Summer
Black bile	Cold and dry	Autumn
Phlegm	Cold and moist	Winter

Red blood was the source of vitality, yellow bile (gastric juice) was necessary for digestion, phlegm (a colorless secretion like sweat or tears) was a lubricant and coolant, and black bile (rarely found pure) was responsible for darkening and thickening the other fluids (as when the blood, skin, or stools turned blackish) (Porter 2002, 38). Health, from a humoral perspective, occurred with the optimal mixture of the humors. Disease was a disturbance of humoral equilibrium, with imbalance in the form of excess, deficit, or inadequate mixture.

Classical physicians' application of this humoral theory to states of depression continues to be a major influence on the way we think about it today. Indeed, the origin of the term "melancholia" comes from the Greek words for black bile, *melas* (black) and *khole* (bile). Hippocratic writings suggest the term melancholia designated several diseases associated with an imbalance of black bile. The aspects most similar to our "depression" involved "despondency, sleeplessness, irritability, [and] restlessness," with autumn being the season of greatest vulnerability, and the brain as the primary organ affected (Jackson 1986, 30). Hippocratic physicians treated melancholia through rebalancing the humors primarily with dietary changes and the oral administration of herbs. Our notions today of "chemical imbalance" carry forward this idea that aspects of the body are out of balance and need physical remedies that seek to restore balance.

Another conceptual legacy of depression from classical times comes from a very different twist put on depression by Plato and Aristotle. Both of these philosophical writers maintain an internal focus, but they are critical of overly medical approaches and articulate a positive side to depression. Plato argues in the *Phaedrus* (370 BC) that madness is not simply medical pathology. Madness can also be a form of inspiration, or what Plato refers to as "Divine Madness." Aristotle's *Problems* (second century BC) picks up the theme of "divine madness" with regard to depression to ask a question that has tremendous resonance in Western history: "Why is it that all of those who have become eminent in philosophy or politics or poetry or the arts are clearly of an atrabilious temperament, and some of them to such an extent as to be affected by disease caused by black bile?" (Aristotle 2000, 57).

The reference to black bile shows that Aristotle is working within a humoral theory. But, for Aristotle, the biological concept bile combines with more psychological and personality concepts. He sees everyone as having some black bile in them: an excess of black bile can be pathological, to the point of depression, but, if the excess does not go too far, it can be salutary and can lead to extraordinary capacities and heights of wisdom. As we will see, during the Renaissance and Romantic period these ideas are developed further and may be said to truly flourish. And, even today, echoes of divine madness, melancholy genius, and salutary depression are important in creative and spiritual models of depression. Also, as we saw, this model is similar to themes raised by the Icarus Project and their conception of depression (and other forms of madness) as "dangerous gifts."

Middle Ages

The Middle Ages and Christianity shifts the emphasis to supernatural variables. The most radical supernatural model of depression from this period revolves around the idea of demonic possession. In this model, people with depression (and madness more broadly) were thought to be possessed by the Devil. A contemporary textbook of psychiatry puts it this way:

> Witches, warlocks, and demons in disguise were very real to the people of the Middle Ages. Various types of misfortune or suffering were often perceived as just punishments meted out through divine intervention as a consequence of sinful behavior . . . Such individuals were often "treated" through the church rather than through medicine, and many were tortured or burned at the stake. The church published texts, such as the *Malleus Maleficatrum* (or the *Hammer of Witches*) to explain how such possessed individuals could be identified and killed.
> (Andreason and Black 1995, 5)

Johann Weyer, a Dutch physician from the sixteenth century, was one of the first to challenge the witchcraft theories that emerged out of the Middle Ages. Through a hybrid model that combined supernatural variables with humoral theory, Weyer argued that most people accused of witchcraft were harmless and should not be punished. It was only "the torture of melancholy [that] makes them fancy that they have caused all sorts of evil" (quoted in Radden 2000, 95). But, for Weyer, this did not exclude a role for the Devil in the process of melancholic thinking. "The Devil," Weyer argued, "loves to insinuate himself into the melancholic humor" (p. 96). Weyer's theory therefore allows for demonic influence and humoral imbalance while at the same time arguing for humane treatment rather than punishment.

Beyond the demonic possession model, another important theory of depression from the middle ages was known as acedia. The concept of acedia developed from the experience of Egyptian desert monks from the fourth century. Articulated by Evagrius Ponticus (AD 345–399) and John Cassian (AD 360–435), acedia was seen as a moral hazard faced by the monks while in pursuit of spiritual growth and connection with God. Evagrius and Cassian understood acedia less as possession and more as a temptation or a vice characterized by "exhaustion, listlessness, sadness or dejection, restlessness, aversion to the cell and ascetic life, and yearning for family and former life" (Jackson 1986, 66). The temptation was thought to be most severe at midday, and so it also went by the name "noonday demon." Cassian describes it as follows:

> Our sixth combat is with . . . [acedia], which we may term weariness or distress of the heart. This is akin to dejection, and is especially trying to solitaries . . . about the sixth hour . . . There are some elders who declare that this is the "midday demon" spoken of in the ninetieth Psalm . . . [W]hen it has taken possession of some unhappy soul, it produces dislike of the place, disgust with the cell, and disdain and contempt of the brethren . . . . [H]e seems worn out and wearied as if with a long journey, or some very heavy work . . . [and] a kind of unreasonable confusion of mind takes possession of him like some foul darkness and makes him idle and useless.
>
> (Cassian 2000, 71–72)

As this description makes clear, acedia overlaps with contemporary depression to a great degree.

Acedia was eventually generalized beyond monks. It came to be linked with the sin of sloth and the moral life of all Christians. Like sloth, acedia was a state to resist. Cassian puts it this way: "the true Christian athlete . . . should hasten to expel this disease . . . from the recesses of his soul; and should strive against this most evil spirit" (p. 73). The importance of acedia as a model of depression is that it introduces the role of willpower. Most models of depression see it as something that happens to people, not something that they can control. But, with acedia, there was a clear moral injunction against giving in to the state of depression. The sufferer was not thought to be under complete control, but through a person's own efforts and through religious confession it was possible to overcome acedia and its temptations (Jackson 1986, 69).

Acedia as a model of depression is very much with us today even though it is rarely called by name. This is particularly true in popular culture where depression is often seen to be a kind of sin or weakness of the will. Similar to the perspective of acedia, this popular perspective assumes that a person should be able to overcome depression with sufficient effort. This approach is controversial and is often critiqued as a source of stigma because it tends to blame the victim of depression for their suffering.

However, there are also recent efforts to revive the acedia model in a more positive light. A good example is Kathleen Norris's compelling memoir, *Acedia and Me*. After a lifetime of struggling with depressive symptoms, Norris found the language of acedia to be more helpful than contemporary languages on depression. On first reading Evagrius and Cassian, Norris "felt a weight lift from my soul, for I had just discovered an accurate description of something that had plagued me for years but that I had never been able to name" (Norris 2008, 4). Norris did not devalue medical approaches and explains that "while I have used medications on occasion, I have found them less helpful than my lifeline of prayers, psalms, and monastic spirituality. When I detect acedia in myself, I do well to muster my resistance" (p. 275). She argues that society loses an important tool for understanding depressive states if it fails to keep the insights of acedia alive.

Renaissance, Enlightenment, and Romanticism

Italian Renaissance humanist, Neoplatonist, medical practitioner, and sufferer from depression, Marsilio Ficino (1433–1499) moved away from notions of depression as possession or acedia. Ficino returned to Greek theories for inspiration, and in his *Three Books on Life*, he mixed together

Hippocrates, Plato, Aristotle and emergent astrological theories to draw together an approach to melancholia that emphasizes the positive value of depression. Along the way, Ficino links black bile, the planet Saturn, exalted moods, intellectual genius, and his own personal experience (Radden 2000, 87–88).

For Ficino, black bile and the planet Saturn are necessary for higher thought: "black bile continually incites the soul to collect itself together into one and to . . . contemplation of whatever is highest, since, indeed, it is most congruent with Saturn, the highest of planets" (Ficino 2000, 90). But, at the same time, the black bile that stimulates higher contemplation leaves learned people, including himself, at risk from depression. If depression becomes too great, artist and philosophers cannot work: "we hope for nothing, we fear everything, and it is weariness to look at the dome of the sky" (p. 92). As a result, Ficino encourages intellectual workers to "temper black bile" through careful attention to diet and activity so that they take advantage of its inspirational effect without falling into depression. Despite this dual edge, Ficino's model of depression is largely positive. Philosophers and artists require melancholia to do their work, and melancholia is a sign of the scholar's success in rising above the small-mindedness of every day life (Solomon 2001, 296).

Spanish Renaissance mystic and poet Saint John of the Cross (1542–1591) also emphasizes the salutary aspects of depression. He draws out the spiritual side of the equation between depression and higher consciousness in his notion of a "dark night of the soul" (or a "dark night" for short). Reminiscent of the Middle Ages concept of acedia, Saint John described a dark night as an affliction of monks characterized by a painful state of spiritual dryness, distance from God, frustration, moral failure, loneliness, impotence, confusion, and despair (Coe 2000, 302). But unlike acedia, and closer to Ficino, a dark night was not a sin or a moral failure. Just the opposite, a dark night was a gift from God and an indication that God felt the person was ready to move to a higher level of spirituality. Saint John describes two types of spiritual dark night—a dark night of the senses and a dark night of the spirit. Each dark night marks a liminal stage of transition from one level of spirituality to the next.

For example, in the first dark night—a dark night of the senses— God withdraws the initial joys of religious life, such as the pleasures of mystical experience, fellowship, purpose, and self importance. This withdrawal can be devastating because these joys are often the main reason for religious practice in the first place. According to St John, people first come to God primarily for the sake of pleasure. Once the spiritual seeker matures beyond these more "immature" needs, God withdraws these pleasures, which initiates the first dark night and ultimately leads to a higher level of spirituality. Professor of Theology and Philosophy, John Coe, describes the process:

> The first dark night opens the way for the major shift or stage of growth (illumination) in which God is loved less for pleasure's sake and more for a love in-and-of-itself. This is a love based upon a real relationship between two persons, more along the lines of a marriage than a romance, or the love between a child and a parent. This in turn leads to the second dark night of the spirit in which the soul must be cured even of wanting God for the sake of experiencing mutual love. Instead, the soul must learn to love God just for Himself in such a manner that He, and not the need to be loved, is the center of all things.
>
> (Coe 2000, 295)

For Saint John, depression, or a dark night, is not a disease or a sin, but a gift, associated with higher levels of spiritual being and consciousness.

In the Enlightenment, these favorable models of depression were eclipsed by a return to more negative versions of depression as medical pathology and biological disease. The biological models that emerge in this period part company from the humoral models that had come before and that had been at the center of medical thinking on depression for nearly 2,000 years, since the time of Hippocrates (Jackson 1986, 116). Dutch physician Herman Boerhaave (1668–1738), who was strongly influenced by Isaac Newton's mechanical principles, moved away from humoral theories in his view of the body as a machine rather than a caldron of humors:

> The human body, then, is composed in such a manner that its united parts are able to produce several motions of very different kinds which derive—fully in accordance with the laws of

mechanics—from the mass, shape, and firmness of the parts
and the way in which the parts are linked together.

(quoted in Radden 2000, 173)

Boerhaave applied his mechanical theory of the body to depression,
and his work can be seen as a transition point in biological theories.
Even though he uses the language of the humors to describe depression,
his causal emphasis focuses on mechanical actions of the blood such
as thickening or slowing. Boerhaave's specific biological theory did not
last, but the Enlightenment approach that he champions will become
dominant in psychiatry's modern period.

Before it does so, however, romantic writers and poets, such as
Johann Wolfgang von Goethe and John Keats, sustain a positive view
of depressive genius and sensitivity that is closer to Aristotle, Ficino,
and Saint John of the Cross. Goethe's *The Sorrows of Young Werther*
(1774) tells the story of young Werther's unrequited love for Charlotte
(Goethe 1971). Werther puts his passion for Charlotte above reason
and prudence, goes through tremendous suffering at the impossibility
of his love, and eventually kills himself out of despair and desperation.
Werther can easily be interpreted as sick or egocentric, but at the same
time the intensity of his feelings (both his love and his suffering) hint
toward a higher consciousness than one can see in "normal" life.

Like Goethe's character Werther, John Keats also goes through
intense suffering as a young man. Not only does he suffer from
unrequited love but both of his parents die by the time he is 15 and
he has an intractable case of tuberculosis that will kill him by the age
of 25. Unsurprisingly, Keats suffers a deep depression. But, rather kill
himself like young Werther, or flee his suffering through drink or
distraction (as others might do), Keats embraces his heartache. In
contrast to what we might expect, Keats does not sink further into
despair or become suicidal. He finds instead a salutary dimension to
his depression, is able to transcend his pain through poetry, and comes
to see a link between death, melancholia, and beauty.

This link between depression and wisdom, or melancholia and
genius, is still with us today. We saw manifestations of it in models
of depression that link sadness to creativity and spirituality. And
contemporary humanist Eric Wilson has recently argued strongly for

a positive dimension to depression in his book *Against Happiness: In Praise of Melancholia*. Wilson combines the tradition of Aristotle, Ficini, and Keats together with a host of contemporary artists, philosophers, and musicians to introduce the term "generative melancholia." For Wilson, generative melancholia "far from a mere disease or weakness of will, is an almost miraculous invitation to transcend the banal status quo and imagine the untapped possibilities for existence" (Wilson 2008, 145).

Like Keats nearly 200 years ago, Wilson asks his contemporaries "Do you not see how necessary a World of Pains and troubles is to school an Intelligence and make it a soul?" (2008, 110). Wilson argues that it is only through enduring and transcending sadness that one can embrace a world where suffering and death are not aberrations. "To deny calamity and the corpse would be to live only a partial life" (p. 110). And, even more, as Keats poem "Ode to Melancholia" attests, to dwell in suffering and death is precisely to dwell in beauty. Things are paradoxically beautiful precisely because they die. Indeed, the two are one: life grows from death, and death from life. For Wilson, "rather than flee from this difficult position, the melancholic appreciates things all the more *because* they die" (p. 113). This is the gift of a generative melancholia.

Modern Times

Modern approaches to depression begin in late nineteenth century Germany with Emil Kraepelin (1856–1926) and the first era of "biological psychiatry" (Shorter 1997, 69).[4] Researchers in this era picked up trends from Enlightenment physicians to argue that "mental illnesses are brain diseases." And they advocated a clinical-pathological research method that extrapolated back and forth between clinical findings and autopsy findings (Fulford, Thornton, and Graham 2006, 152; Porter 2002, 144; Shorter 1997, 73–76). Kraepelin brought this method to international attention when he used it to set up a psychiatric department in Munich that included such neurological and psychiatric luminaries as Alois Alzheimer, Franz Nissl, and Korbinian Brodmann.

Kraepelin's department was the nodal point for a period of tremendous optimism in psychiatric research during the early decades of the twentieth century. Researchers during this time firmly believed that systematic use of the clinical-pathological method would discover brain abnormalities that lay behind major psychiatric conditions. Their optimism was fueled by the neuropathological discovery of two organic mental disorders: Alzheimer's disease and general paralysis (syphilis of the brain). These last two discoveries were "world changing" events— "for the first time a specific psychiatric disease had been shown to have a specific neuropathological cause"—and the race was on to replicate similar findings throughout psychiatry (Fulford et al. 2006, 152).

Kraepelin's approach to depression also contributed to the excitement. His success articulating a clinical distinction between dementia praecox (later called schizophrenia) and manic-depressive insanity (later bipolar disorder) has become a staple of psychiatric thinking. This distinction between "thought disorders" and "mood disorders" is still used today, and the popularity of the category "manic-depression" is largely responsible for our more frequent use of the term "depression" relative to the term "melancholia" (despite the fact that Kraepelin still used "melancholia" when talking about depression). Kraepelin's depressive states were carefully differentiated into four groups. The first of these, "Melancholia simplex," was dominated by a mood of "profound inward dejection and gloomy hopelessness" with marked anhedonia: "the patient's heart is heavy, nothing can permanently rouse his interest, nothing gives him pleasure." Thinking problems in melancholia simplex were limited to negative thoughts consistent with a depressed mood and difficulties in concentration and sluggishness: "He cannot collect his thoughts or pull himself together . . . his head [also] feels heavy, quite stupid . . . everything is confused" (Kraepelin 2000, 261).

The other three categories were "melancholia gravis," "paranoid melancholia," and "fantastic melancholia." Melancholia gravis was melancholia with hallucinations and delusions. Paranoid melancholia was also melancholia with delusions and hallucinations, this time with paranoid themes that were otherwise coherent and logical. And, finally, fantastic melancholia was melancholia with abundant and fantastical hallucinations: "the patients see evil spirits, death, heads of animals, smoke in the house, black men on the roofs, crowds of monsters, lions' cubs, a grey head with sharp teeth, angels, saints, dead relatives . . ." (Kraepelin 2000, 271).

This meticulous diagnostic approach has led to Kraepelin being called the "father of modern psychiatry" because his classifications prefigures today's Diagnostic and Statistical Manual (often referred to as the "bible of psychiatry"). Similar to contemporary biological psychiatrists, Kraepelin very much hoped his diagnostic precision would lead to neuropathological correlates like the ones for syphilis and Alzheimer's. Despite this hope, however, further research at the time yielded little in the way of useful findings. The first era of biological psychiatrists pressed on nonetheless, undaunted by their limited findings. They pushed so hard and the biological models they adopted eventually became so fantastic that their colleagues started condescendingly referring to them as "Brain Mythologies" (Fulford et al. 2006, 153). By the late 1920s, alternative approaches gained increasing attention, and the first era of biological psychiatry lost its pride of place.

The most influential alternative was Sigmund Freud's psychoanalysis. Freud, who was born the same year as Kraepelin, started out as a neurologist and early on he also hoped that brain science would explain psychiatric problems. But he eventually had to abandon this goal, in large part because he was forced into clinical practice (rather than academic research) to make a living. In private practice, Freud had to develop methods of treatment rather than simply do research. "Anyone who wants to make a living from the treatment of nervous patients," Freud explains, "must clearly be able to do something to help them" (Freud 1959, 16). The only treatments available were electrotherapy and hypnotism. Freud found electrotherapy to be completely unhelpful, so he turned to hypnotherapy and eventually to "psycho-analysis."

Freud's turn to psychoanalysis was a historic choice because it meant that he had to "abandon the treatment of organic nervous diseases" (1959, 17). Leaving behind his earlier research in neurology, Freud worked instead to understand his patients' experiences. He put the same painstaking attention into understanding the interpretive links of his patient's psychic life as the biological psychiatrists had put into cataloguing symptoms and examining brains. Freud's psychoanalysis flourished, and he developed a series of insights into human psychic life that were hard to ignore. Concepts such as repression, resistance, mental conflict, ambivalence, unconscious, conversion, free association, infantile sexuality, libido, transference, dream work, manifest verses, latent dream content, the Oedipal Complex, narcissism, and ego, id, and superego became the lingua franca of not only psychiatry but also the era. And, as we saw in our discussion of contemporary models of depression, Freud's approach to depression as pathological mourning continues to be influential in psychoanalysis today.

Freud's psychoanalytic model of depression opens the door to the host of contemporary psychotherapeutic approaches we have already reviewed in Chapter 2. These many psychotherapy options for depression were developed partly by psychiatry, but also by social workers, counselors, art therapists, and psychologists. In these latter fields, they continue to flourish. In psychiatry, there was some interest in these models of depression, particularly cognitive-behavioral approaches, but by 1980 the field had largely turned away from psychoanalysis and psychotherapy back toward biopsychiatry. 1980 marks the watershed year because this was the year the American Psychiatric Association published its new *Diagnostic and Statistical Manual of Mental Disorders*, 3rd ed. (*DSM-III*). The manual decisively and purposefully returns to Kraepelin and the first era of biological psychiatry. True to this desire, historian of psychiatry Edwin Shorter explained years later that *DSM-III* signaled a "turning of the page on psychoanalysis" and "a redirection of the discipline toward a scientific course" (Shorter 1997, 302). We reviewed the modern scientific approaches to depression that followed this turn to biology in Chapter 1. In Chapter 5, we will consider some of the cultural dynamics surrounding the turn.

Conclusion

Psychiatry's return to Kraepelin and the disease model of depression brings us back to the present moment. The disease model dominates our thinking on depression, but it exists alongside a host of additional models that are still very much alive. All of these contemporary models have echoes of previous approaches in history. Social and political models of depression are reminiscent of ancient times and the idea that people feel bad when bad things happen to them. Biological and disease models go all the way back to Hippocratic writings and the humoral theory of depression. Psychological models have their antecedents in the tragic plays of Greece. Religious models such as possession and acedia gained favor in the Middle Ages. And generative melancholia, which lives on in creative and spiritual models of depression as well as in the approaches of many consumer activists, goes back to Plato and Aristotle with further flourishing in the Renaissance and Romantic period.

The historical record on depression defamiliarizes our common sense notions. It reveals how unlikely it will be for a single model to ever capture the "truth" of depression. The longevity of the models also reveals that each perspective must contain important wisdom about the human condition. To lose or to collapse models would be to lose important insights about human suffering. In some ways, the longevity of the many models of depression leaves us in a situation similar to the Indian parable of the blind men and the elephant that was captured by John Saxe's memorable poem, "The Blind Men and the Elephant":

It was six men of Indostan
To learning much inclined,
Who went to see the Elephant
(Though all of them were blind),
That each by observation
Might satisfy his mind.

The *First* approached the Elephant,
And happening to fall
Against his broad and sturdy side,
At once began to bawl:
"God bless me! but the Elephant
Is very like a WALL!"

The *Second*, feeling of the tusk,
Cried, "Ho, what have we here,
So very round and smooth and sharp?
To me 'tis mighty clear
This wonder of an Elephant
Is very like a SPEAR!"

The *Third* approached the animal,
And happening to take

The squirming trunk within his hands,
Thus boldly up and spake:
"I see," quoth he, "the Elephant
Is very like a SNAKE!"

The *Fourth* reached out an eager hand,
And felt about the knee
"What most this wondrous beast is like
Is mighty plain," quoth he:
"'Tis clear enough the Elephant
Is very like a TREE!"

The *Fifth*, who chanced to touch the ear,
Said: "E'en the blindest man
Can tell what this resembles most;
Deny the fact who can,
This marvel of an Elephant
Is very like a FAN!"

The *Sixth* no sooner had begun
About the beast to grope,
Than seizing on the swinging tail
That fell within his scope,
"I see," quoth he, "the Elephant
Is very like a ROPE!"

And so these men of Indostan
Disputed loud and long,
Each in his own opinion
Exceeding stiff and strong,
Though each was partly in the right,
And all were in the wrong!

(Saxe 1873, 135–136)

From this perspective (assuming that different approaches to depression always remain partially blind to aspects of the world), all we can do is get different takes on depression that illuminate different aspects of the phenomenon. Each different approach gives important information, but none is complete in itself since depression is too multifaceted for any one approach to fully capture the whole. This perspective is helpful because it allows us to appreciate different models while at the same time remaining humble about them and without dogmatically insisting on a single correct perspective.

In other ways, things are even less clear and even more humbling. At least in the parable of the blind men and the elephant there is a single elephant independent of human ideas that the men are all researching (even if they do so from very different perspectives). But with depression, the idea that there is a single entity that everyone is studying seems unlikely. It is much more likely that the phenomenon of depression does not exist as a single entity outside of the ideas we use to make sense of it. Instead, depression and our ideas of depression co-constitute each other. This means there is no single depression from which we have different perspectives. It is more likely that there are multiple phenomena called depression bound up in the multiple perspectives from which we try to understand them.

Historian and philosopher Michel Foucault made this insight vividly clear in a simple yet profound observation from his *History of Madness* (Foucault 2006). Foucault pointed out that the cohesion of the symptoms we think of as melancholia and depression likely was co-constituted through humoral theory. Before the emergence of humoral theory there was no concept of melancholia or depression. Indeed, the conception of depression was first imagined through the logic of humoral theory, not the other way around. We did not start with "depression" and then use humoral theory to explain it. Rather, we started with humoral theory and organized our observations of people through the lens of the theory, which, in a circular fashion, we then used to explain to ourselves. It is true that we can see a cluster of depressive symptoms in earlier times (prior to humoral theory), but the story of Gilgamesh (for example) does not organize Gilgamesh's suffering along the lines of what we think of as melancholia or depression. That is a retrospective diagnosis. It would be possible to diagnose Gilgamesh as depressed only after the emergence of the idea of "melancholia" which allowed depression to become a topic in Western history.

Foucault helps us understand this initial co-constitution of depression and humoral theory through his insight that the symptoms associated with depression and the qualities of black bile are uncannily similar. The depressive symptoms of "sadness, darkness, slowness . . . [were] perceived as a certain qualitative coherence" by an unconscious logic of black bile (dark, sluggish, heavy) that shapes the very organization, selection, and perception of depressive traits (Foucault 2006, 265). Black bile, originally a bodily concept, gets transferred as an organizing concept for making sense of human emotions. The emotions are real, but they do not come pre-packaged in particular syndrome clusters. We have to create these clusters into categories that we use to think with. Both our categories and our explanations get all tangled up with our conceptual theories. As a result, depression, Foucault suggested, is not discovery and not mere social construction. It is something "half-way between the two" (2006, 265). Depression is a symbolically organized interaction with the real that goes back to Hippocratic writings and forward to today's multiple models of depression. Each model not only has a different understanding of depression but also pulls out from the reality of human emotions different clusters to focus on and to explain. Once again (only even more so) we are left in a situation where we can appreciate the models without becoming dogmatic about them. What is fascinating about Foucault's insight is that without an initial theory of black bile, we might never have become preoccupied with the constellation of symptoms we now consider depression.

As humbling as Foucault's insight might be for any hope of "truly" understanding the essence of "depression" (how to characterize it, what to distinguish it from, what causes it, how to treat it), the next chapter will show that history is not the only way to defamiliarize our thinking on depression. Like historical exploration, turning our attention to cultural dimensions of depression is invaluable for putting contemporary Western approaches in perspective.

4 Cultural Context

The study of depression across cultures reveals tremendous variability of experience, labeling strategies, and healing approaches. Cultural study therefore reinforces our appreciation of the diversity models, and it helps us recognize the tremendous plasticity of experience that can be associated with depression. It provides a window into how depression is open to cultural change, and it helps us see how powerful social actors can influence cultural perspectives. This chapter uses a cultural perspective to look at anthropological and cross-cultural psychiatric insights into the variability of depression. In addition, we get a behind-the-scenes look at the role pharmaceutical marketing practices play in shaping worldwide cultural experiences of depression. Finally, we use this information to reflect back on the culture of psychiatry in the U.S. and the rise of the biomedical model in psychiatry.

Cultural Diversity

Anthropological research reveals diverse sources of misery around the world, multiple interpretations of suffering and despair, and a diversity of physiological reactions, interpersonal connections, religious practices, and collective identifications associated with depression. In their classic collection *Culture and Depression*, Arthur Kleinman and Byron Good provide examples of these anthropological findings: "the Ifaluk have no concept of depression as joylessness, the Kaluli have no concept of depression at all, Thai peasants take a religious not an illness perspective on prolonged grief, and [as we saw in the last chapter] in medieval Europe the sadness of sloth and acedia and the humors of melancholia merge" (Kleinman and Good 1985, 37).

Cross-cultural psychiatrists frequently find that depression can be experienced in somatic terms rather than emotional terms. In "somatizing cultures," as one textbook explains, "depressive experiences may be expressed as complaints of weakness, tiredness, 'imbalance' (Chinese and Asian cultures), 'nerves' and headaches (in Latino and Mediterranean cultures), or being 'heartbroken' (among Hopi Native American culture)" (Gaw 2010, p. 6 of online copy). "Soul loss or spirit loss" is also a common way to express depression in many cultures. In these cultures, the model of depression involved implies that the person has "somehow lost or been abandoned by the indwelling source of energy and vitality that animates the healthy person" (Kirmayer and Jarvis 2006, 704).

An issue that often comes up in the face of this cultural diversity is the question of universality of psychopathology or "cross-cultural equivalence" of symptoms (Kirmayer and Jarvis 2006, 700). Following this concern, cross-cultural psychiatry has tried to find a single medical entity underlying wide ranging experiences. Cultural psychiatrist Arthur Kleinman uses the distinction between "illness" and "disease" to help frame this concern: "*illness* refers to patient's perception, experience, expression and pattern of coping with symptoms, while *disease* refers to the way practitioners recast illness in terms of their theoretical models of pathology" (Kleinman 1988, 7). The problem with the search for universality comes when either disease or illness are reified as entities to be discovered underneath layers of cultural camouflage. This easily creates what Kleinman calls a "category fallacy," where researchers fail to recognize that disease logics and illness logics are both cultural constructs (Kleinman 1977, 4). To avoid this kind of category fallacy we must recognize the unlikelihood of stripping away of layers of cultural accretion in order to isolate a culture-free entity of illness or disease.

Cultural anthropologists have pointed out that category fallacy problems often complicate epidemiological studies (including the studies I cited in the first chapter). When one culture takes its own culturally constructed symptom clusters and applies it to other cultures, they often find the symptom clusters in the new culture. But if the target culture does not think in terms of these same symptom clusters, the finding has little meaning in that culture. To illustrate the tautological reasoning contained in many epidemiologic studies, cultural anthropologists Gananath Obeyesekere develops a thought experiment using what he playfully calls "reverse ethnocentrism."

Obeyesekere asks us to imagine the case of a South Asian male who has the following symptoms: drastic weight loss, sexual fantasies, and night emissions and urine discoloration. "In South Asia," Obeyesekere explains, "the patient may be diagnosed as suffering from a disease 'semen loss.' But on the operational level I can find this constellation of symptoms in every society, from China to Peru" (Obeyesekere 1985, 136). Similarly, using operational criteria of the "disease," one could "prove" that plenty of Americans suffer from the condition of semen loss. No one in American culture would take you seriously, however, because even though the symptoms exist they have not been fused into a conception of semen loss. If the cluster of symptoms does not exist as a conception in the new culture, that cluster of symptoms is neither disease nor illness. It is nonsense.

Obeyesekere points out, however, that not all cross-cultural comparisons end up in nonsense. Sometimes they result in sharp conflicts of meaning. For example, in Sri Lanka, a Buddhist culture, depressive affects (sadness, pessimism, sorrow) do exist together. But this cluster of feelings is also organized into a rich cultural heritage that means they are resistant to being organized into the metaphors of a disease model. Depressive feelings in Sri Lanka are culturally generalized through a Buddhist world view and given spiritual significance. Personal feelings of loss and sadness are triggers that help people appreciate wider philosophical and religious truths of impermanence, craving, and suffering inherent in the nature of things. Obeyesekere notes that depressive feelings are so valued for understanding these Buddhist truths that meditative practices are designed specifically to initiate them. Once they arise, depressive affect and hopelessness are generalized into "an ontological problem of existence, defined in its Buddhist sense as 'suffering'" (Obeyesekere 1985, 139). Awareness of suffering from this perspective is viewed positively as wisdom.

Depression and Global Pharmaceuticals

Cultural difference clearly complicates epidemiological study of depression and can create disorienting conflicts of meaning, but it is also important not to idealize the concept of culture. Early anthropologic usage of the term culture emphasized shared patterns of meaning that define social groups. This usage is helpful but it can also be problematic because, as Kleinman reminds us, it tends:

> to portray cultures as bounded, fixed entities, neglecting crucial differences among and within groups, and it risked reducing culture to an autonomous variable among others. But culture

is not one thing; it is a process by which ordinary activities acquire emotional and moral meaning for participants.

(Kleinman 2004)

The reminder that culture is not a "thing" but is a "process" is particularly important for making sense of a globalizing world where cultural processes are in rapid in flux.

Foregrounding culture as a process allows us to appreciate not only cultural difference but also cultural change. Scholars in cultural anthropology and in interdisciplinary domains such as cultural studies have long been aware that culture is a fluid process and have made a point to study cultural change (Clarke, Mamo, Fosket, Fishman, and Shim 2010; Davis and Morris 2007; Lewis 2007; Martin 2007; Rose 2003). But, more than scholars, the group that has been most influential in this regard has been marketing practitioners (Applbaum 2004). Transnational pharmaceutical marketers have used an awareness of cultural plasticity not only to study cultural change but also to create cultural change in the experience of depression (Petryna, Lakoff, and Kleinman 2006). The paradigm example involves recent transitions in the culture of depression in Japan.

Epidemiologic studies of depression in Japan consistently show lower rates compared with the West. For example, the World Health Survey Initiative estimated a twelve-month prevalence of mood disorders to be around 3.1% in Japan compared with 9.6% in the U.S. (WHO World Mental Health Survey Consortium 2004). These reduced rates of depression in Japan can be explained by a number of factors (Kirmayer 2002). One of the most important factors is stigma. Until recently Japan focused its psychiatric care on severe disorders, and this practice reinforced a severe stigma associated with psychiatric conditions. Another factor is that, unlike in the West, the concept of "depression" does not have an established place in Japanese culture. People with experiences in the range of depression tend to be understood as having psychosomatic or anxiety problems and treated by family physicians or internist rather than mental health specialists. In addition, as Obeyesekere found in Sri Lanka, Japan's Buddhist heritage creates a positive valuation of depression relative to the West. Anthropologist Margaret Lock describes the positive valuation of depression in her classic study of Japan:

Feeling sad and reacting sensitively to losses, particularly of loved ones, is an idea that has a singular appeal in Japan. The theater, a range of literature and indigenous popular songs, traditional and modern, positively wallow in nostalgia, sensations of grief and loss, and a sense of the impermanence of things . . . [And] sadness, grief, and melancholy are accepted as an inevitable part of human life and even welcomed at times for their symbolic value, as a reminder of the ephemeral nature of this world.

(Lock 1993, 222–223)

All of these factors come together to create very low rates of depression in Japan.

These lower rates of depression are well known in the pharmaceutical industry. Indeed, through most of the 1990s Eli Lilly decided against selling Prozac, its serotonin reuptake inhibitor (SSRI), in Japan despite the fact that the drug was a huge blockbuster elsewhere. Lilly made this decision because of the high cost of drug approval in Japan (particularly for a drug with questionable efficacy that might fail to be approved) combined with market research showing low incidence of depression. The two factors made the cost/benefit equation seem unfavorable (Applbaum 2006, 89; Schulz 2004). Smaller manufacturers followed the industry leaders. Solvay Pharmaceuticals, the maker of the less popular SSRI Luvox, explained their decision not to enter the Japanese market in everyday language. They reported on their website in 1988: "Japan is very hesitant about anti-depressant drugs. That is mainly because of the culture" (Vickery 2010, 379). In other words, cultural resistance to the concept of depression was too great to sell antidepressants in Japan.

But, during this same period (the 1980s and 1990s) the pharmaceutical industry became so adept at creating cultural change that by the turn of the century it no longer hesitated to bring SSRIs to Japan. The cultural challenge the pharmaceuticals faced when they finally decided to enter the Japanese market was immense. It required the pharmaceutical companies to work together to "alter the total sales environment" for the drugs (Applbaum 2006, 87). This meant doing a systematic analysis of what marketers call "cultural obstacles" in an effort to turn the Japanese sales environment into something resembling the U.S. The key cultural obstacles were "public recognition and acceptance of mental illness in scientific terms, progressiveness of the insurance system, infrastructure for the distribution of SSRIs, national and personal income to pay for them" (p. 101). In addition, there also needed to be a culture of brand recognition, free market pricing, prescriptions on demand, and prescriptions written by non-specialists (especially in Japan where there are fewer psychiatrists). It is clear that to achieve cultural change goals as wide as these the pharmaceuticals had to reach far more people than psychiatrists. They also had to target patients, clinicians, government bureaucrats, journalists, and hospital administrators, just to name a few.

Pharmaceutical marketers have found that they can catalyze this kind of cultural and institutional change through a wide reaching "educational" campaign. These educational campaigns, or more accurately promotional campaigns, stimulate consumer demand for the product, and they stimulate cultural demand for the institutional change needed to distribute the product (Applbaum 2006, 101). There is by now a well researched (and fairly standard) pharmaceutical industry playbook for these kinds of promotional campaigns that can be applied from one country to the next (Angell 2005; Applbaum 2010; Healy 2004; Moynihan, Heath, and Henry 2002; Rose 2006). The playbook was developed in the West and its basics were then transferred to Japan. The easiest way to dissect the pharmaceutical marketing playbook is to articulate four lines of promotion: direct-to-consumer; direct-to-provider; indirect-to-consumer; and indirect-to-provider.

The most well-known tool in the pharmaceutical marketing playbook for U.S. readers is *direct-to-consumer* (DTC) advertising that now saturates U.S. media. The avalanche of DTC advertising in the U.S. began with a rules change in 1997, when the Food and Drug Administration allowed drug companies to advertise without the prior restrictions on full disclosure of side effects (Angell 2005, 123). The result was that spending on direct-to-consumer advertising grew from 266 million dollars in 1996 to 2.6 billion dollars in 2001 (Greider 2003, 88). Japan does not allow DTC promotion, but the pharmaceutical industry was able to get around these restrictions through a number of ingenious moves (Applbaum 2004). One tactic was to place full-page advertisements for clinical trials that feature information on depression and a branded imprint of the company's drug (clinical trial ads were not regulated like DTC ads). The pharmaceuticals also distributed glossy waiting room brochures in doctors' offices around the country with the same information. And they developed internet sites where patients could simultaneously be educated about depression and SSRI treatment. This last tactic was so effective that one Tokyo marketing manager argued that the Web was the best way to achieve DTC advertising:

> The web basically circumvents DTC rules, so there is no need to be concerned over these. People go to the company Web site and take a quiz to see whether they might have depression. If yes, they go to the doctor and ask for the medication.
>
> (Applbaum 2004, 63)

Direct-to-provider (DTP) promotion consists of a corresponding campaign to directly influence clinicians. DTP promotion tactics include a barrage of advertisements placed in clinical journals, the creation of "throw away" journals as a vehicle for additional adverts, direct mailing campaigns to swamp clinician's mailboxes with adverts and promotions, and drug adverts placed on banners and billboards at conference sites. DTP also takes the form of medical representatives (or "drug reps") who go to the physician's office or hospital to promote pharmaceutical products. Company managers and corporate trainers study physician prescribing patterns, their concerns over side effects, and their needs with regard to patient complaints. Managers combine this prescribing research with information about the drug and spin it into a prepared script for drug reps that favorably shapes the information: "Every *objection* (by physicians, patients, and the general public) can be turned around to become a *positive* selling point, something to be valued and sold for the patient's benefit" (Oldani 2004, 328). The drug reps become remarkably adept at this type of "spin selling" (or "spin doctoring"). In addition, drug reps create an unspoken gift exchange economy by providing clinicians with a variety of gift tokens, including pins, paperweights, clocks, note pads (all of which carry the drugs adverts), along with meals, trips, sporting events, and free samples. All of these gifts not only promote the drugs, they increase the likelihood that the prescriber will return the gift through their prescribing practices. Although we know a great deal more about these drug rep practices in the West, there is every reason to believe they work similarly in Japan (Saito, Mukoharaz and Bito, 2010).

Indirect promotion practices (to both consumers and providers) are less well known because they are much less obvious. Yet, indirect strategies are arguably the most effective strategy for the pharmaceutical industry because they catch the consumer and provider off guard. These indirect strategies are like the magician's second hand—the first hand (direct promotion) distracts the viewer while the second hand (indirect promotion) performs the magic trick outside the viewer's awareness. These indirect methods follow the basic public relations tactic known as the "third man" technique—where promotion comes indirectly through a seemingly neutral "third man" and therefore sidesteps the usual scrutiny and skepticism people give to direct advertising and promotion (Rampton and Stauber 2002). Also indirect promotional practices tend to fall in the category of what critics call "disease mongering." In disease mongering, the medical treatment is not sold, but rather the disease itself. The idea is that the more people that know about the "disease" the more the treatment will be sold: "Disease mongering can include turning ordinary ailments into medical problems, seeing mild symptoms as serious, treating personal problems as medical, seeing risks as diseases, and faming prevalence estimates to maximize potential markets" (Moynihan et al. 2002).

Indirect-to-consumer (ITC) practices commonly consist of press and video news releases, celebrity endorsements, product placement techniques, and the setting up and/or funding of various patient and disease specific advocacy groups (which allow products to be promoted without it seeming like it comes from the corporations directly). In Japan, some examples of ITC include sponsoring the release of numerous books on depression, constant media discussions of depression, distribution of Crown Princess Masako's acknowledgement that she was on antidepressants, lavish funding of anti-stigma campaigns, and depression awareness campaigns that teach consumers the basic symptoms and treatments of depression through a disease model (Shulz 2004). Awareness campaigns require the pharmaceutical marketers to devise culturally specific models for the condition. Since Japan has no concept of mild to moderate depression as a disease, the pharmaceuticals devised and introduced the notion that your "soul can have a cold" (*koroko no kaze*). And, if your soul does have a cold, it will need pharmaceutical treatment (Mills 2007; Shulz 2004).

Indirect-to-provider (ITP) practices consist of an avalanche of promotion in the form of continuing education materials, key psychiatric opinion leaders, and psychiatric practice and treatment guidelines (Applbaum 2009). Even psychiatric science itself has now become a marketing arm of the pharmaceutical companies (Sismondo 2007, 2008; Smith 2005). All of these professional materials provide ideal "third man" resources because people have strong assumptions of neutrality regarding these sources, particularly scientific articles in professional review articles. To get inside the science of medicine and psychiatry, pharmaceuticals not only ghostwrite scientific articles, they often ghost manage the entire research process including decisions about what questions to ask, what methods to use, what counts as outcome, and which studies are released (Healy 2006, Sismondo 2007, 2008). Some basic tactics for designing marketable research include using:

> comparator drugs that may be administered at a too-low dose, so that the sponsor's drug looks more effective, or at a too-high dose, so that the sponsor's drugs have relatively fewer adverse side effects . . . downplaying serious adverse effects . . . [and] comparing a new drug with placebo when the relevant question is how does it compare with an old drug.
>
> (Angell 2008, 1070)

Using these practices, industry-sponsored research can consistently support the company's marketing agenda.

In Japan, the use of these direct and indirect promotional tactics proved to be a resounding success in just a few years. "Between 1998 and 2003 sales of antidepressants in Japan quintupled . . . GlaxoSmithKleine alone saw its sales of Paxil increased from $108 million in 2001 to $298 million in 2003" (Schulz 2004). A Japanese company spokesman found that during one seven-month ad campaign it ran in 2003, 110,000 people consulted their doctors about depression—a phenomenon that would have seemed unbelievable just ten years earlier.

The Pharmaceuticals and the Shift to Modern Scientific Psychiatry

This discussion of pharmaceutical marketing practices in Japan reflects back on the culture of psychiatry in the U.S. It helps us understand why the disease model is so prominent in the U.S. and why psychiatric science tends to focus on disease model approaches. The pharmaceutical industry is global, but the major world market is in the U.S. and pharmaceutical practices are particularly influential in this country.

Marcia Angell, the former editor and chief of *The New England Journal of Medicine* and the author of *The Truth about Drug Companies*, explains that the year 1980 is a pivotal year for understanding pharmaceutical industry. Before 1980 the pharmaceutical industry "was a good business, but afterward it was a stupendous one" (Angell 2005, 3). Drug sales were fairly steady from 1960 to 1980, but during the next twenty years sales tripled to more than $200 billion a year (Angell 2005, 3). The year 1980 is the watershed year for the pharmaceutical industry because in one sweep it brought the election of Ronald Reagan, a new business-friendly climate in congress, and the passage of several pro-business legislations (such as the Bayh-Dole Act designed to speed technology transfers from tax-supported universities to the corporations). In the wake of these changes, the pharmaceutical industry unleashed a promotional blitz of staggering proportions. And this promotional blitz was where the marketing playbook of direct and indirect promotional strategies were fully developed and mastered.

The history of the pharmaceutical industry is critical to understanding the U.S. transition to disease model psychiatry because the year 1980 is also a pivotal year for psychiatry. Recall that when we discussed the history of psychiatry, 1980 was the watershed year for the reemergence of biopsychiatry and the disease model. It was the year that the *DSM-III* was published, and this event heralded the transition from psychoanalysis to biopsychiatry. The transition of the pharmaceutical industry into a corporate colossus at the same time as psychiatry moved into its second biological era is not a coincidence. The rise of the pharmaceuticals transformed the "ethos of medical schools and teaching hospitals. These non-profit institutions started to see themselves as 'partners' of industry and they became just as enthusiastic as any entrepreneur about the opportunities to parlay their discoveries into financial gain" (Angell 2005, 8).

All of medicine was targeted, but psychiatry in particular provided an ideal site for pharmaceutical attention. During the years of pharmaceutical growth there were very few new cures developed. The vast bulk of the increased drug sales after 1980 were lifestyle drugs and me-too drugs devoted to chronic conditions. This meant psychiatry was the perfect focus for pharmaceutical growth because psychiatric conditions tended to be chronic lifestyle conditions with fuzzy boundaries that are particularly open to marketing tactics. Not surprisingly, psychiatric drugs have led the list of pharmaceutical best sellers during this period, and psychiatry has provided pharmaceutical public relations experts with a corporate "marketer's dream" (Angell 2005, 88).

During this period marketing and the research aspects of pharmaceutical companies have not been separate. Since 1980, the pharmaceuticals have transformed themselves from "research-driven companies" to ones that operate "more like Procter & Gamble, the maker of Tide" (Matheson 2008; Petersen 2000). This makes sense because in order to expand their markets for chronic lifestyle conditions such as depression, marketing executives rather than scientists had to be in charge. The industry had to move away from a focus on product per se and towards the creation of climate of opinion and desire surrounding the product. Jan Leshley, the former CEO of Squibb pharmaceuticals, explains the move companies had to make using the analogy between "software" and "hardware":

> Suddenly information technology was so essential that we realized we are an information company more than we are a pill company. Because it's the software—all the research, networking, marketing—that's important in a pill . . . It's not the pill that costs so much it's the software.
>
> (quoted in Crister 2005, 61)

In Leschley's analogy, the modern colossal drug company does not sell its products, the pills, as much as the information that surrounds their pills. Today's pharmaceutical industry has become an information industry, an industry of cultural change, not a pill industry. At a global level, the whole world has been and will continue to be impacted. At a professional level, as we saw in Chapter 1, psychiatry has been transformed into a narrow scientific research enterprise that focuses primarily on the disease model, neuroscientific variables, and pharmaceutical treatments.

Conclusion

Adopting a cultural approach to depression reveals that the experience of depression varies tremendously according to cultural context. The phenomenon of cultural diversity also reveals a cultural plasticity that is the springboard for global pharmaceutical efforts to transform depressive states into profits. Diverse cultural experiences of depression can be reconfigured into a disease model and a pharmaceutical treatment. Global pharmaceuticals have become remarkably adept at doing just this. Indeed, more than providing medical cures, cultural change on this magnitude is at the heart of contemporary pharmaceuticals' business plans. The spin doctoring and cultural-change skills that have emerged from these business plans are tremendous, and around the world diverse approaches to depression are converging into a disease model. Along the way, psychiatry itself has been transformed into a biomedically oriented discipline that emphasizes broken brains and pharmaceutical treatments.

PART III
THEORETICAL AND CLINICAL CONCERNS

5 What We May Never Know

The diversity of models of depression in our time and historically, together with their plasticity across cultures and the role of powerful social actors to create dominant models, can only leave us humble with regard to the "true" meaning of depression. In the face of such multiplicity of models and their inextricable historical and cultural context, depression no longer seems simply a disease. Just the opposite, depression seems inescapably malleable, opening itself up to a range of possible meaning formations and lived experiences. Furthermore, with all this diversity, we do not know which of the many models of depression, or which combinations of models, is best for ourselves and for our loved ones. We will likely never know.

Yet we must respond to depression. Depression requires us to make choices about how to understand it and how to intervene. But we have no definitive guideline for these choices. There is no single doctor to whom we can turn to tell us what to do. As a result, those of us touched by depression in our own lives or in the lives of our loved ones (which includes almost everyone) need sophisticated tools for navigating depression in the face of uncertainty. There are very few resources within the models of depression that can provide us with such tools. In this chapter, we turn to theory and philosophy for guidance in the face of this conundrum.

There are many ways we could do this, but perhaps the most helpful way to bridge models of depression with fine-grained personal and clinical choices is through narrative theory. Narrative theory helps us understand how we story our lives. It offers a rich language for understanding how linguistic frames and metaphorical structures get incorporated into lived experience and personal identity. And, with regard to depression, narrative theory helps connect the dots between clinical models such as biopsychiatry and psychoanalysis, and the intimate details of our life stories. It helps us see how people use and, in some ways, are used by available models to make sense of their lives and the lives of others.

Narrative Theory

Narrative scholars articulate the elements of narrative in a variety of ways, and it would take an entire treatise on narrative theory to sort them out. But we can get helpful hints on how to begin by turning to clinicians who have found narrative theory useful in their work.[5] Clinicians find that the narrative elements most essential for clinical encounters are *metaphor, plot, character* and *point of view*. The first of these, metaphor, is particularly crucial for navigating models of depression because as we will see a model of depression is a kind of metaphor of depression. But metaphor is just one of the many tools of narrative. In the following section, we will review each of these four elements of narrative and then bring them together to discuss their relevance for the many and varied ways sadness is told or narrated.

Metaphor

The stories people tell about themselves and others are rich with metaphor. Common sense would tell us that these metaphors have little importance since metaphor in most people's minds does little more than embellish or add ornamentation to the content of a story. But for influential literary theorists such as I. A. Richards, a number of philosophers, particularly Max Black, Mary Hesse, Paul Ricoeur, and Mark Johnson, and increasingly for cognitive scientists such as George Lakoff, metaphor has a much larger function. In their book *Metaphors*

We Live By, Lakoff and Johnson put it most succinctly: "metaphor is not just a matter of language, that is, of mere words . . . On the contrary, human thought processes are largely metaphorical" (Lakoff and Johnson 1980, 6). They argue that metaphor is a pervasive aspect of human life, not just in the words that we use but also in our very concepts. "Our ordinary conceptual system, in terms of which we both think and act, is fundamentally metaphorical in nature" (1980, 3). By shaping our concepts, metaphor structures the way we perceive the world, what we experience, how we relate to other people, and the choices we make. It even organizes diverse cultural and sub-cultural approaches to suffering and healing (Kirmayer 2004).

Metaphor performs this function by allowing us to understand and experience one thing in terms of something else. Hesse uses the example, borrowed from Black, of "man is a wolf" (Hesse 2000, 351). Hesse explains that the metaphor works because it transfers ideas and associations from one term to the other. The metaphor selects, accentuates, and backgrounds aspects of two systems of ideas so that they come to be seen as similar. As Hesse puts it, "Men are seen to be more like wolves after the wolf metaphor is used, and wolves seem to be more human" (2000, 351). Through metaphor, the two terms, or more precisely the two systems of terms, interact and adapt to one another.

Metaphors are the key to understanding the many models of depression because metaphors and models work in similar ways. In ordinary writing or conversation, people use metaphors to provide a quick glimpse. But with a model, research communities (e.g. biomedical, psychoanalytic) develop the metaphor into a systematic model that frames their research. These scientific models explain the world through a metaphorical re-description (Hesse 2000, 353). Just as "man is a wolf" re-describes man in a new way and allows us to perceive something new about him, so too the disease model of depression—"depression is a disease"—re-describes sadness and allows us to perceive something new about it. Philosophical psychiatrists Bill Fulford and Tony Colombo use these insights to develop the following definition of psychiatric models: "[Psychiatric] *models* . . . are the conceptual frameworks, or sets of ideas, by which, in any given area, people structure and make sense of the world around them" (Fulford and Columbo 2004, 130).

This definition sidesteps controversy around "social construction" versus the "real world" in psychiatric modeling. It allows us to understand that the constraints of the real world contribute to model choice in the sense that the real world accommodates and resists different model options. One cannot simply use any old model. But, at the same time, the real world is complex enough that it accommodates a variety of models. This means that model choice is also a value choice. Choosing models of depression requires us to determine which variables are the most important to us because different models foreground different variables. Disease models foreground biology, psychoanalytic models foreground loss, family models foreground the family, etc. Even integrative models such as the biopsychosocial model have to choose which models to integrate and they have to choose the relative emphasis to give the models chosen.

Philosopher of science Ronald Giere provides a helpful discussion of how model choice in physics navigates between the values and the real world:

> Models need only be similar to particular real world systems in specified respects and to limited degrees of accuracy. The question for a model is how well it "fits" various real world systems one is trying to represent. One can admit that no model fits the world perfectly in all respects while insisting that, for specified real world systems, some models clearly fit better than others. The better fitting models may represent more aspects of the real world or fit some aspects more accurately, or both. In any case, "fit" is not simply a relationship between a model and the world. It requires a specification of which aspects of the world are important to represent and, for those aspects, how close a fit is desirable.
>
> (Giere 2000, 186)

Giere makes it clear that model choice, even in physics, is a human interpretive practice made in the face of uncertainty and particular value choices. Model choice in depression as in physics simultaneously requires fidelity to the real world, judgment and choice regarding which aspect of the world matters, and wisdom (informed by trial and error) in decision making.

Plot

Plot works like metaphor in that plot also orders our experience and provides form to our narratives. Plot brings together what would otherwise be separate and plot organizes our temporal perception. The organizing function of plot is that it creates a narrative synthesis between multiple elements and events and brings them together into a single story. With this function of plot it is possible to have understandable stories composed of wildly diverse and disparate parts. For example, human thoughts, human desires, unplanned accidents, other people's thoughts and desires, divine intervention, natural laws, economic downturns, the weather, and cell phones (just to name a few) are all easily brought together through the process of "emplotment." Without a plot, we have no way to make sense of such wildly diverse phenomena.

In addition, plot is essential for human meaning because plot configures the multiple elements of narrative into a temporal order that is crucial for our experience of time. Philosopher Paul Ricoeur sees the relation between time and plot as a two-way phenomena: time makes sense to us precisely because it is organized by plot, and conversely, plot is meaningful because it portrays the features of temporal experience (Ricoeur 1984). Both plot and human time are organized in a temporal order composed of three parts: beginning, middle, and end. Without plot we cannot make sense of time, and only because we have a plotted sense of time do we understand emplotment. Ricoeur admits that his conclusion is "undeniably circular," but he argues that this circularity is "not a vicious, but a healthy circle" (1984, 3). Emplotment, from this perspective, can be seen as a kind of prosthetic device. It does not solve the riddle of time so much as it allows us to keep going by leaning on the prosthesis of plot.

Character

Character in narrative theory brings us into contemporary controversies over basic concepts of self and identity. The controversy around what it means to be a self involves a tension between essentialist and non-essentialist approaches. On the one hand, essentialist notions of identity tell us that we have a fixed personality, perhaps biologically stamped, that is authentically ours, and that is at the core of our being. This "true self" or "core self" may be distorted or covered over, but it is none the less there for the discovery if we apply ourselves patiently and persistently to the task. On the other hand, a variety of non-essentialist critiques have deconstructed this ideal of identity and its notion of an integral, original, and unified self. Non-essentialist approaches argue instead for a much more social and linguistically constructed understanding of self and identity.

One of the most productive ways to navigate the tension between essentialist and non-essentialist understandings of identity has been to draw a comparison between identity in life and character in fiction. This approach uses a comparative logic to argue that we understand ourselves the same way we understand characters. Ricoeur calls this approach *narrative identity*: "fiction, in particular narrative fiction, is an irreducible dimension of self-understanding . . . fiction is only completed in life and life can be understood only through the stories that we tell about it" (Ricoeur 1991, 30). Self-understanding, on this account, is an interpretive event and narrative is the privileged form for this interpretation: "a life story [is] a fictional history or, if one prefers, a historical fiction, interweaving the historiographic style of biographies with the novelistic style of imaginary autobiographies" (Ricoeur 1992, 114).

Literary theorist Peter Brooks sums up narrative identity beautifully in his book *Reading for the Plot: Design and Intention in Narrative*:

> Our lives are ceaselessly intertwined with narrative, with the stories that we tell and hear told, those we dream or imagine or would like to tell, all of which are reworked in that story of our own interrupted monologue. We live immersed in narrative, recounting and reassessing the meaning of our past actions, anticipating the outcome of our future projects, situating ourselves at the intersection of several stories not yet completed.
>
> (Brooks 1984, 3)

Narrative approaches to identity allow us to navigate the tension between essentialist and non-essentialist identities because narrative identity allows for continuity over time, a relative stability of self, without implying a substantial or essentialist core to this stability. The stability of our narrative interpretations comes not from an individual essence but from the weight of the stories we tell about ourselves.

Bringing metaphor, plot, and character together, we can say that when models of depression seep from the clinic into the culture, they become part of our cultural resources of self-experience. In times of trouble, we look through the metaphorical structures of mental models to perceive, select, and plot aspects of our lives that we believe to be important. These culturally located "self" stories and the priorities within those stories combine with other cultural stories to scaffold our narrative identity and provide us with a compass for living. They tell us where we have been, where we are now, and they provide us with a trajectory into the future.

Point of View

This power of models and plots to shape our narrative identity brings us to *point of view*. As we have seen, when different people look through different models of depression, they come up with different points of view. When those different points of view are organized into life stories, they yield very different narrative identities. If a person with depression sees a clinician who is working from a disease model, the therapist will perceive the person's depression and provide treatment recommendations consistent with that model and with the aspects of that model that they prioritize. The perceptions, treatment recommendations, and narrative identifications that form will be very different if the person sees a psychoanalyst or a family therapist, or starts taking creative writing classes. The therapist working in the disease model will see a broken brain and recommend some form of biological intervention, the psychoanalyst will see loss and unconscious psychic conflicts and will recommend psychodynamic therapy, the family therapist will see dysfunctional family patterns and will recommend family work, and the creative writing teacher will see an undeveloped muse that needs further discovery and expression.

Each of these different people uses the structure of metaphor (and the models those metaphors become) to organize very different points of view. If the person struggling with depression adopts one of these points of view, then she will come to see herself in the light of that point of view. But if she adopts a different point of view, then she will see herself very differently. Either way, what she does next and the treatment she finds reasonable to pursue, will come from the point of view she inhabits.

Stories of Sadness

The implication of narrative theory is that there are many ways to tell the story of sadness. There is not just one right way and many other wrong ones. All the models of depression involve a process of story telling and story re-telling. No matter which model one uses, the process of healing involves an initial set of problems that the person is unable resolve. The client and therapist use one or more models of depression to bring additional perspectives to their problems, which allows the client to understand them in a new way. The perspectives vary greatly depending on which model of depression is used. But from the vantage point of narrative theory, what these different approaches all have in common is that they re-work, or "re-author," the patient's initial story of sadness into a new story. This new story allows new degrees of flexibility for understanding the past and provides new strategies for moving into the future.

An awareness of the narrative dimension of *all* models of depression —and thus an understanding that does not see models of depression as inherently "right" or "wrong"—fits well with an ethical approach to clinical work that philosophers of psychiatry refer to as values-based-practice (VBP). The first principle of VBP gets to the heart of the issue: "All [clinical] decisions stand on two feet, on values as well as on facts, including decisions about diagnosis (the 'two feet' principle)" (Fulford 2004, 208; Fulford et al. 2006, 498). The first principle of VBP means that data and evidence alone cannot determine clinical decisions or choices of diagnostic models. Even in cases where there is good data to support a clinical model and intervention, that alone does not determine the decision. The final decision still depends on how the intervention lines up with the person's life choices, life goals, and narrative identity (who they want to be).

Bill Fulford gives an example of an artist who ultimately decides against taking lithium for mood swings even though there was good data to support the use of lithium medication (and even though it did help to calm her instability). The artist makes this decision because lithium reduced her capacity to visualize color. For her, the effect of lithium on her experience of color was more important than its effects on her moods. Using narrative theory, we can say that the artist preferred to "diagnose" and intervene in her problems through a creative/expressive model rather than a biomedical one. Data alone could not determine this decision (Fulford 2004).

Seeing models of depression as elements of equally valuable narratives also fits well with consumer activist concerns regarding psychiatry. For the last thirty years consumer activism in psychiatry has worked to break the paternalistic power structures of clinical encounters (Lewis, 2006b). Recently, this consumer movement has blossomed into a robust "recovery coalition," which has flourished in community psychiatry settings (Sowers and Thompson 2007). A major force driving the recovery coalition is the increasing chorus of criticism against psychiatric insistence on one-dimensional disease models, much of which is fueled by the pharmaceutical industry as we discussed in Chapter 4. The criticism comes not only from consumer activists but also from critical mental health providers, and interdisciplinary academics working at the interface of psychiatry, disability studies, and cultural theory (see www.mindfreedom.org; http://theicarusproject.net:, Bracken and Thomas 2005; Double 2006; Lewis 2006a; Morrison 2005; Tamini and Cohen 2008).

The heart of the recovery coalition centers on shifting psychiatry from a structure of "experts know best" to one of "service user control." As medical anthropologist Kim Hopper summarizes, the recovery movement primarily concerns "reworking traditional power relationships, conferring distinctive expertise on service users, and rewriting the mandate of public mental health systems" (Hopper 2007, 868). In recovery, therefore, the emphasis shifts from "objective knowledge" to "lived experience." Recovery approaches are less interested in the "truth" questions surrounding mental illness and more interested in the experience of people who are different or who have troubles. Thus, the key questions from a recovery perspective move from "Where is it broken?" to "How can I be of help?"

In all of these dimensions, recovery creates a shift away from the centrality of "experts"—professionals, academics, researchers, codes of practice, training courses and university departments. In the standard "expert" paradigm, "service users might be consulted and invited to comment on the models and the interventions and the research, but they are always recipients of expertise generated elsewhere" (Bracken 2007, 401). By contrast, in recovery approaches, service users are considered the true experts. They are the ones who most understand the challenges in their lives of psychic difference and psychic suffering – these challenges often involve unique and deeply personal experiences of sanism (prejudice against the psychically different) and exclusion, power and coercion, and mental health care system dysfunction and disinterest. In addition, they are the ones who most know the context of their own situation and their own value preferences. They are the ones who should make choices regarding how to prioritize those values. And they are the ones to decide who they wish to be.

This does not mean that recovery oriented approaches reject professional services or contributions. It simply means that professional contributions become potentially helpful resources rather than necessary dictates. As recovery oriented psychiatrist Patrick Bracken puts it:

> The most radical implication of the recovery agenda, with its reversal of what is of primary and secondary significance, is the fact that when it comes to issues to do with values, meanings and relationships it is users/survivors themselves who are the most knowledgeable and informed. When it comes to the recovery agenda, they are the real experts.
>
> (2007, 402)

And, when it comes to depression, the only person who can ultimately narrate our sadness is us.

Conclusion

The many models of depression leave us with the question of how to navigate choices between them. Through narrative theory we can see that the model choice is also a life choice, because the model (or models) that we choose to understand our depression will shape what we do next and even how we understand ourselves. By working through the theoretical questions around the multiple models of depression, we can see that we have choices in understanding our depression, and we can also see what the consequences of those choices will be. This may seem abstract from a theoretical perspective, but when we turn to clinical situations it is all too real. In the next chapter we will discuss the choices of clinical encounters to help us concretize and apply the issues we have discussed with regard to depression.

6 Clinical Encounters

We now have a wealth of material from which to consider depression. We have looked at multiple models of depression, and we have worked through the historical, cultural, and theoretical dimensions of depression. Along the way, we have learned that there are many ways to understand depression and that each of these options have something to offer. We have learned that decisions between alternatives cannot be reduced to questions of science, or facts, alone. Each model contains a world view that highlights the facts that matter, and each model contains a set of value preferences about the role of suffering in human life. Decisions about models of depression are "two feet" decisions that rest on facts and values and the inevitable intertwining of the two. As a result, decisions people make about their depression are not simply "medical" or "psychiatric"—they are deeply personal choices through which people understand their lives, narrate their identity, and decide how they wish to live.

Our next step is to see what these insights mean for clinical encounters and for the many choices people inevitably make in the face of depression. To do this, we start by looking closely at a fictional portrayal of depression and its treatment. We follow with a consideration of psychotherapy outcome studies and with qualitative research findings from people who have recovered from depression. We conclude with a reading of depression memoirs.

Ordinary People as Case History

The fictional case we will work with comes from the 1980 Academy Award winning film for best picture, *Ordinary People*. I choose this film because of its rich characterization of depression, and because it is accessible and a pleasure to watch. If you have not had a chance to see *Ordinary People*, I encourage you to do so now (if possible before going forward with this chapter).

We can begin our discussion of the film by outlining its basic plot structure (Guest 1976; Schwary and Redford 1980). Conrad, the film's protagonist, suffers from depression during his junior year of high school. The depression is precipitated by his brother's death in a boating accident. The depression becomes so severe that Conrad attempts suicide by locking himself in the bathroom and slashing his wrists. After the suicide attempt, Conrad is hospitalized, treated with electroshock therapy, and discharged back home to re-enter high school and live with his parents (his father is a tax attorney and his mother is a homemaker). At his father's insistence, Conrad begins out-patient treatment with Dr. Berger—a local psychiatrist. Conrad uses an early visit to request medication help for controlling his feelings, but Dr. Berger refuses this request. Indeed, Berger dismisses this option with a sarcastic remark: "I think you came in here looking like something out of The Body Snatchers. It's not my impression that you need a tranquilizer." Rather than medication, Berger recommends twice-weekly psychotherapy and Conrad agrees.

Dr. Berger does not discuss which model of psychotherapy he is recommending, but as the film unfolds it becomes clear that he uses a psychoanalytic approach similar to the one we discussed in Chapter 2. The goal for Dr. Berger is just the opposite of Conrad's initial goal of emotional control. Dr. Berger encourages Conrad to explore his feelings and to gain greater access to them through free association. Berger and Conrad use this exploration and increased awareness to uncover unconscious dimensions of Conrad's sadness. During their work together, it becomes clear to them that Conrad's depression comes primarily from his unresolved grief over his brother's death. Conrad's grief has been interrupted by a number of factors, including his general tendency to suppress his feelings (in pursuit of control), his guilt for not saving his brother (Conrad held on to the capsized boat after his brother fell off), and his residual anger at his brother for being irresponsible and for letting go of the boat.

In addition to losing his brother, the main additional loss that comes up in therapy involves Conrad's relationship with his mother. Throughout Conrad's life his mother has been distant and emotionally aloof toward Conrad. This comes largely from her own tendencies to control emotion and partly from her deep admiration for Conrad's brother—who was always much more outgoing and socially successful than Conrad. The loss of his mother's affection, in relation to how Conrad would wish for her to be, is also a source of grief for Conrad. During the therapy he works through this loss as well and comes to understand and forgive his mother for being who she is rather than his childhood fantasy of her.

The film ends on an ambivalent note. On the one hand, Conrad makes tremendous progress. He has resolved many of his sad feelings and come to a better peace with his mother. He has started dating, has found new activities he enjoys, and has developed new coping methods for handling emotions (which are more flexible than his previous tendencies to deny and repress his feelings). But on the other hand, the family as a whole falls apart. The tension between Conrad and his mother improves, but the tension surrounding his mother and the family does not disappear. Instead, the tension migrates from Conrad to his father—with the result that his father falls out of love with his mother and his parents decide to separate. In the last scene of the film, his mother moves out of the house and his father explains to Conrad their plan to separate and live apart.

Understanding Conrad's Choices

If we use *Ordinary People* as a case history, it is helpful to wind the film back to the moment when Conrad first goes to see Dr. Berger. The many models of depression mean that psychoanalysis was not the only choice available. It would have been possible for Conrad to use a range of different approaches. He could have stayed with his initial goal of "controlling" his feelings through the use of medications and a disease model. He could have pursued the goal of control through a cognitive behavioral model that might help him correct his "cognitive distortions" and the sad feelings that can flow from these. He could have taken a much more family oriented route that might have better addressed the marital relationship and therefore avoided the separation of the parents. He could have worked with a feminist therapist who might have helped him understand that much of his mother's problems can be understood through a gendered frame (patriarchic culture has forced his mother into maternal-feminine roles that are a very poor fit for her). Or he could have avoided therapy altogether, as he initially wished, and used non-therapeutic options such as religion, politics, or creative expression.

Considering the historical and cultural context in which *Ordinary People* was produced, it is not surprising Dr. Berger recommended psychoanalysis with very little discussion of other options. The original book by Judith Guest came out in 1976, and the film version was released in 1980 (the threshold year for U.S. psychiatry). Guest likely started writing the book in the early to mid 1970s, which would place the film historically and culturally in the last years of psychoanalytic dominance. This would be particularly true for upper middle class Americans. A person such as Conrad from a wealthy suburb of Chicago who was seeking out-patient therapy for depression during those years would almost certainly have received psychoanalytic treatment. Psychoanalysis would have been so prevalent in that context, and its world view so naturalized, that other options would not have been discussed.

What is fascinating is how rapidly this situation has changed. If *Ordinary People* was set today, Conrad would just as assuredly receive medications and a disease model diagnosis. As in the 1970s, very few other options would be discussed. That does not mean that other options have disappeared; it just means that they are not in the mainstream of clinical practice. A contemporary Dr. Berger would therefore most likely work with Conrad to find a medication that would be helpful. In addition, common to today's standards of care, he might also recommend cognitive-behavioral therapy (CBT) to go with it. In a similar way to Conrad beginning treatment with Dr. Berger, neither the medication nor the CBT would come with a discussion of alternatives. They would be naturalized as the obvious and the only treatment recommendation worth talking about.

It might seem on first consideration that a medication and CBT combination would have been an inferior treatment option for Conrad compared to psychoanalysis. The film makes Conrad's progress through psychoanalysis so compelling that it is hard to see other options as viable. But from a theoretical perspective, it is likely that other treatment options could also have been effective for Conrad. Other options would have certainly been different from psychoanalysis; as such they would have had some losses relative to psychoanalysis, but they would also have had some advantages over psychoanalysis.

For example, it is possible that a disease model combined with CBT would have been more consistent with the way that Conrad's mother thought about the whole situation. And it is possible that if Conrad had gone that route, the family might not have been as disrupted as it was through psychoanalysis. Or to take another example, based on Conrad's inclinations it seems like creative expression might have been his first choice rather than psychoanalysis. He does not seem drawn to therapy at first (even though he eventually takes well to being in therapy), and it is clear from the film that music has a major healing effect for Conrad. From the perspective of creative expression as a healing practice, Conrad could have chosen to seriously immerse himself in his music. If he had taken this path, rather than the formal treatment option, Conrad could have used creative expression as a way to work through and cope with his feelings in a new and more helpful way.

Using our conceptual work from Chapter 5, we can see that the main issue is not which model of depression is superior but which one Conrad most wishes to use. Each model could be effective in helping Conrad make sense of his past and his present, and each model could give him direction for the future. But the differences of narrative identity between the models would vary considerably. This becomes particularly true when we open up to the many additional models that are available to Conrad beyond psychoanalysis, disease model, and CBT to include humanistic, family, spiritual, creative, and political models as well. In the end, the choice between these many models should not belong to the clinician. The choice should belong to Conrad. It is his life, not the clinician's life. Conrad should be able to decide to which approach he feels most drawn. If Conrad were to become a danger to himself or to others, his clinician might have to pursue involuntary hospitalization to ensure his safety. But short of this, it is Conrad who should make decisions about his life.

This does not mean that all of the possible options will necessarily be helpful—only that any one, or combination, might be helpful, and the choice should be Conrad's rather than the therapist's. Since Conrad is inclined in the creative expression direction, that gives it some advantage were he to go that route, but, still, it is also possible that the first choice Conrad makes will not be helpful. He may have to try something else instead, or combine approaches. Certainly, the film gives a good example of a "case" where a couple of options are not helpful. Conrad's friend from the hospital, Karen, finds formal therapy (we do not know which type) unhelpful, particularly since her father is very against it. Karen soon drops out of therapy, but then she also does not find a creative expression option helpful either: we know from the film that she continues in a production of "A Thousand Clowns." Shortly after this, Karen goes on to attempt and complete suicide, so, clearly, creative expression did not work for her (although just as clearly she seems likely to have been going through the motions of being in the play rather than really investing herself in the dramatic arts).

What seems most important to understand is that insights from a variety of models to depression allow new forms of freedom and flexibility emerge, but as Karen's situation highlights, there are no guarantees. Nor does taking multiple models seriously embrace "anything goes" relativity that would allow us to simply make up any story we like in order to understand our situation. Instead, it creates a conceptual scaffold where ontological questions (such as "What are the core features of psychic life?") and epistemological questions (such as "What is the best method to study and treat people?") are not fixed in advance. Different answers may emerge depending on related ethical questions (such as "What kind of people do we want to be?" and "What kind of life-worlds do we want to create?"). Different understandings of the core features of people and different methods of inquiry and treatment of depression yield very different kinds of people with very different life experiences. There is no absolute way that people must choose because there are multiple ways to organize human life. Nor is there a guarantee that all or any approaches will fit a particular individual. Making judgments between these different ways largely depends on the consequences and desired values. In short, there are multiple paths to wisdom and a meaningful life.

As a result, any number of different interpretations of Conrad's sadness could possibly be developed and worked through in a therapeutic relationship with a quality, well-meaning practitioner. Or if it were outside the clinical frame, this kind of working through could happen in mentoring relationships in a spiritual, creative, or political practice. In either case, there is a very good chance that an array of different insights and narrative structures could effectively help Conrad understand his sadness and provide him with tools for feeling better. If the insights and narrative frames were not imposed on him but were ones that he participated in creating and felt strongly connected to their meaning, the therapy or other transformative practice would "work" through encouraging modifications in Conrad's assumptive worlds. These modifications would diffract and reconfigure the meanings of his sadness in more favorable directions and free him up for alternative forms of coping.

From Fiction to Reality—Psychotherapy Outcome Studies

There are a variety of empirical supports for this reading of Conrad's story. Starting with psychotherapy outcome studies, psychiatrist Jerome Frank provides a good overview of this research in his book *Persuasion and Healing: A Comparative Study of Psychotherapy*:

> My position is not that technique is irrelevant to outcome. Rather, I maintain that . . . the success of all techniques depends on the patient's sense of alliance with an actual or symbolic healer. This position implies that ideally therapists should select for each patient the therapy that accords, or can be brought into accord, with the patient's personal characteristics and view of the problem. Also implied is that therapists should seek to learn as many approaches as they find congenial and convincing. Creating a good therapeutic match may involve both educating the patient about the therapist's conceptual scheme and, if necessary, modifying the scheme to take into account the concepts the patient brings to therapy.
>
> (Frank and Frank 1991)

Frank's finding that alternative psychotherapies are all *equally effective* is known in the therapeutic research community as the "Dodo effect."

This affectionate appellation comes from a line in *Alice in Wonderland*: "At last, Dodo said, everyone has won and all must have prizes" (Rosenzweig 1936, 412).[6]

Although this finding is not universally accepted and has been minimally integrated into clinical practice, empirical studies confirm with remarkable consistency that the positive effects of therapy (of which there are many) are not due to the specific interventions of the therapist. The benefits of therapy come instead from common factors of the therapeutic setting. These studies suggest that the process of setting up a therapeutic relationship with a quality therapist who is kind, empathic, and experienced is much more important than the content of the specific models and theories from which the therapist works. The Dodo effect insight arose out of psychotherapy research, but since the difference in outcome between antidepressants and placebos is small, there is good reason to believe that the Dodo effect applies to medication therapy as much it does to psychotherapy (Greenberg 1999; Sparks, Duncan, Cohen, and Antonuccio 2009).

The implication of the Dodo effect is that a variety of theoretical models can be used to understand, to cope with, and to ameliorate painful emotional states. The Dodo effect does not mean that any old interpretation will do. For psychotherapy to be effective the therapist and the client must have a sense of belief and confidence in the frame being used. In the words of Saul Rosenzweig, who first coined the Dodo effect:

> Whether the therapist talks in terms of psychoanalysis or Christian Science is . . . relatively unimportant as compared with the formal consistency with which the doctrine employed is adhered to, for by virtue of this consistency the patient receives a schema for achieving some sort and degree of personality organization.
>
> (Rosenzweig 1936, 413–415)

It follows that for the therapist to apply the model consistently, they must believe in the model. In addition, for the client to make use of the model, there must also be a fit between therapist and client. The single most important non-specific factor in therapeutic work is a sense of rapport and alliance between therapist and client (Duncan, Miller,

Wampold, and Hubble 2009). If the therapist uses an approach that does not fit with the client's world view, rapport between therapist and client quickly falters. This means that more than one model—from psychoanalysis to Christian Science—can be helpful even though any particular model necessarily simplifies the situation. But for it to "work," both the therapist and the client must invest in the model, and they must find it plausible and valuable. By investing in a model or combination of models, the therapist and client work through the implications of that model (or combination of models) for the person who is suffering. Applying this insight to depression, each of the different approaches to depression may be seen as care and practice of the self. Each becomes a way of bringing into being a certain kind of subjectivity and developing a particular narrative identity.

The results of a recent qualitative study on depression recovery is consistent with this perspective. Damien Ridge and Sue Ziebland interviewed 38 men and women who had previously experienced depression to discover the strategies they used to revitalize their lives following depression (Ridge and Ziebland 2006). Ridge and Ziebland found that the people they interviewed did not use any single approach. Instead, they selected a variety of "narrative tools," such as talking therapy, medication, yoga, and complementary therapies to regain mastery of their situation. Ridge explains: a "key finding . . . was that recovery tools considered effective by patients go hand in hand with telling a good story about recovering from depression" (Ridge 2009, 174). The very process of assembling a range of tools for recovery helped create the stories that were effective. The people interviewed found that therapists were most helpful if they could function not as experts but as "recovery allies." The most helpful health professionals were those who were empathic and good listeners, provided hope and encouragement, and who had a positive belief in the person going through the depression. A recovery ally of this type does not function in a "doctor knows best" capacity, but is someone who helps the person select the narratives and the recovery tools that feel most true to them.

Memoirs of Depression

Over the last few years there has been a surge of memoirs devoted to depression. These memoirs provide a wealth of empirical information regarding how people actually understand and cope with depression. For a quick glimpse into this work consider the following titles: *Darkness Visible: A Memoir of Madness, Prozac Nation: Young and Depressed in America, Songs from the Black Chair, Poets on Prozac: Mental Illness, Treatment and the Creative Process, Undercurrents: A Therapist's Reckoning with Her Own Depression, Manhattan, When I Was Young, Unholy Ghost: Writers on Depression, The Beast: A Journey through Depression, What's Normal? Narratives of Mental and Emotional Disorders, Illness in the Academy: A Collection of Pathographies by Academics, Return to Ithaca, Acedia and Me: A Marriage, Monks, and a Writer's Life, Lost in America: A Journey with My Father, In Love with Daylight: A Memoir of Recovery, Prozac Diary,* and *Speaking of Sadness: Depression, Disconnection, and the Meanings of Illness.*

Hillary Clark, an English professor who studies depression memoirs, finds that depression, if it is serious, is not simply an isolated life event. Depression becomes central to a person's sense of themselves and their identity formation. "One cannot feel well one day, numb and oppressed the next, suicidal after a few months have elapsed," and go through the arduous process of trying to cope with these and many other symptoms of depression "without seeking a narrative explanation—the cycle of bipolar disorder, for instance, or the Christian narrative of sin, repentance, and redemption—in order to make sense of it all, to trace a single self through all these changes" (Clark 2008, 2).

For Clark, we should listen to memoirs and other personal narratives of depression on their own merits rather than using them to impose normative diagnoses or treatment regimes. Personal narratives "give voice to the ill, the traumatized, and the disabled," and restore the insights and wisdom they have achieved—wisdom that is often lost by medical research, which turns people into diagnostic labels and statistics (Clark 2008, 3). This way of listening is similar to the way anthropologists listen when they visit a new culture. Anthropologists put their judgments on hold, they keep their ethnocentrisms at bay, they bracket their preconceived notions, and they try to understand a way of life from inside that way of life—how it makes sense, what advantages it has for the people who live that way of life, and how it has integrity of its own. Following these suggestions, we can use examples from two particularly rich collections of depression memoirs for further reflection: *Unholy Ghost: Writers on Depression* (Casey 2002) and *Poets on Prozac: Mental Illness, Treatment and the Creative Process* (Berlin 2008).

In "Planet No," from *Unholy Ghost*, Lesley Dormen emphasizes themes of loss and depression through a model of unresolved grief similar to Conrad's story in *Ordinary People*. Dormen explains that her life was first sent spiraling into depression by two losses: "An architect I'd loved for under a year left me for a woman he met in a supermarket parking lot. And my best friend, Tessa, a woman as central to my understanding of myself as my brown eyes and small feet, disappeared into marriage and withdrew from our friendship completely" (Dormen 2002, 229). As in Conrad's story, these losses are explored in psychoanalytic therapy, and Dormen comes to realize that they have been compounded by earlier childhood losses. She lost her father after her parents divorced when she was six, she was sexually abused by her stepfather, and she had a complicated emotional relationship with her mother. When her therapist asked her "if [you] were a girl in a story, how would [you] see yourself," she answered: "Like an orphan" (p. 252). The many ungrieved losses in her life amplified each other, and the feelings were with her in the present as much as the past. She re-lived the experience not only in her past losses but also in the solitary isolation and sense of failure she felt as an unmarried woman in New York.

Through therapy and self-reflection she came to understand her stepfather's sexual abuse of her was "the curve in [her] depression story. His touch had caused the spine of the story to veer off into a new direction, had reconfigured the terms of my loves and longings" (Dormen 2002, 268). Most pernicious for her ongoing development, her stepfather's abuse left her confused about her desires, and this confusion left her "frozen in a girlhood made curiously old" (p. 249). The dense and painful emotional intensities that grew up around the sexual abuse knotted together shame, illicit sexual pleasure, heartbreaking loss, pity, betrayal, guilt, duplicity, and an aching distance between her mother and herself. These knots were so tight that she could not begin to open them or untie the feelings, but at the same time she could not forget them. She found herself constantly and repeatedly returning to them "with the vague uneasiness that was a familiar part of [her] internal landscape" (p. 232).

Slowly and often painfully, therapy helped her move past these knots in her character that seemed to rope her into depression and despair. She was able to separate herself from this history. "Something happened—something that was separate from me. There was a me that existed before the something and a me that existed after. Before and after were separate, not the same" (p. 238). Now that she was no longer tied together in knots, "it was possible to stand outside those events, to observe them and draw a conclusion about them. It was possible not to just be them" (Dormen 2002, 238). Not only that, it became possible to move past the grief, to feel joy, and to make new connections:

> I fell in love with New York, with the giddy green of the first spring after the worst of the depression lifted, with new friends, travel, and wonderful books. I looked around my apartment and saw that there was pleasure in things, in their colors and shapes, and that one did not actually need a marriage certificate to buy good pots.
>
> (Dormen 2002, 240)

By contrast, William Styron's memoir excerpted from *Darkness Visible*, is paradigmatic of the disease model as a narrative template. Styron describes himself as "laid low by the disease," a "major illness" of "horrible intensity," which came on him like a "brainstorm . . . a veritable howling tempest in the brain, which is indeed what clinical depression resembles like nothing else" (Styron 2002, 114–115). This connection between depression and bad weather perfectly captures the disease model approach to depression as lying outside the frame of human goals, desires, losses, and disappointments. Like the weather, depression comes from the material world of inhuman forces and physical and chemical interactions. For a strong disease model advocate, it makes no more sense to give human meaning to depression than to say to an atheist that thunder is because the Gods are angry with us. Styron explains how he sees it: "I shall never learn what 'caused' my depression, as no one will ever learn about their own . . . so complex are the intermingling factors of abnormal chemistry, behavior and genetics" (p. 115).

Styron's memoir is one of the first and most influential to adopt this narrative frame, and he relies on the chemical imbalance theory to explain the disease. Depression, he decides, "results from an aberration of biochemical process. [It] is chemically induced amid the neurotransmitters of the brain ... a depletion of the chemicals norephineprine and serotonin" (Styron 2002, 120). This "upheaval in the brain tissues" causes the mind "to feel aggrieved, stricken," and it creates "muddied thought processes" like the "distress of an organ in convulsion" (p. 121). But Styron is not alone in his approach; the disease model runs through many of the other memoirs as well. Virginia Hefferman laments her "substandard physiology" which creates her depression (Hefferman 2002, 20). Chase Twichell chimes in with an updated theoretical explanation: "What happens in depression, for reasons that are still unknown is that the limbic-diencephalic system malfunctions" (Twichell 2002). And Russell Banks fears that his wife's "malfunctioning limbic diencephalic systems" may result in her suicide (Banks 2002).

It is interesting to compare the disease model of depression with an unresolved grief model. One way to do this is by comparing Lesley Dormen's memoir (discussed above) with Liza Porter's memoir, "Down the Tracks Bruce Springsteen Sang to Me" (Porter 2008). Many of the same themes arise in Porter's memoir that arose Dormen's memoir—loss of best friend, excruciating breakups, sexual abuse, complicated childhood, and psychotherapy. But for Porter the primary narrative frame through which she understands herself is the disease model. After years of battling depression, she sees a psychiatrist who convincingly explains to her: "You've been clinically depressed most of your life and have never been properly treated for it" (p. 157). The psychiatrist goes on to "explain brain chemistry, dopamine, serotonin reuptake inhibitors," and he says, "I'll be able to help you. You may not feel better right away, and we might have to try many different medications, but I'll help you" (p. 157). Even before they try any medications, Porter is dramatically relieved by the psychiatrist's pronouncement of depressive disease:

> I raise my head and stare at him. I weep. And I believe him
> ... Finally I admit powerlessness. This is the first time I ever

truly realize that it is not my fault; there is nothing more I can possibly do to fight the depression . . . I have an actual physical disease . . ., and there is treatment for it. I quit trying to convince myself that I have to fix it, or even that I can fix it. I decide to trust this doctor to help me find the right medications. Hope is back.

(Porter 2008, 157)

This hope sustains Porter through three long years of medication trials:

We go through Wellbutrin, Celexa, Effexor, Zoloft, Ritalin, Lamictal, Provigil, and Seroquel. More drugs I can't remember the names of, but I do recall the side effects—Zoloft gave me the shits, Effexor had me jerking and twitching in the night, Lamictal constipated me . . . Almost all the drugs steal my sex drive. But something starts happening in my brain, I feel better.

(Porter 2008, 157)

And gradually, through a combination of Wellbutrin, Lamictal, and Ritalin, Porter comes to the other side of depression. "The depression and its voices recede into the background. I become able to write poems about things other than my sordid past" (p. 157). She finds that she becomes more mature and more focused through "changes in [her] brain chemistry." Her writing—something she has always enjoyed and has used to cope with her feelings— begins to change as well:

After the antidepressants begin to work, my [writing] becomes more universal. Others besides me can relate to it. I have energy to submit poems to magazines. Editors begin accepting them. I learn—as a writer friend has told me several times—to turn the hardships of my life into beauty.

(Porter 2008, 158)

Gravitating toward neither a disease model nor a psychoanalytic one, David Budbill approaches his painful periods of depression through a spiritual and creative frame. Perhaps because of what he calls his "rebellious, contrary" nature, none of the mainstream approaches was suitable for him. Instead, he developed his "own way of dealing with and using depression" that he calls his "give in" method:

> I discovered that the only way around my periods of depression is directly through them; in other words, the sooner I can resign myself to the Angel of Depression, the sooner she will be done with me and leave me alone.
>
> (Budbill 2008, 83)

Drawing insight from Zen Buddhist teachings, Budbill found that if he let go of his critique of depression and allowed himself to be with the intensity of the feelings, they were not all negative. Indeed, depression could be generative. Budbill found that one of the most important positive dimensions of depression was that it slowed him down. Depression forced him to enter a "negative space" where he could not work or be productive; instead he had to tune into a very different experience—"empty, open, quiet, passive, receptive, dark" (p. 89). These slothful, withdrawn periods functioned as a kind of dormancy where he could store up energy for times when the Angel of Depression let him go. During this time, he could better hear his muse than he could when he was not depressed, and this "receptacle" period would later emerge in his poetry.

Susanna Kaysen also takes a generative approach to her depression. In "One Cheer for Melancholy," she explains, "I think melancholy is useful" (Kaysen 2002, 38). It tunes people in to fundamental contradictions of life: "failure, disease, death" are all standard life events. "Is it any surprise," she asks, "if some of the time, some of us feel like hell?" Kaysen does not frame her generative melancholia through a spiritual or creative model, but through an evolutionary model. She speculates that the reason there is so much depression in the world is that it provides balance. "I've learned this from my optimistic friends. I rely on them and their cheerful attitudes. Together, we make a complete picture. My doom and gloom may be more often right, but they aren't the whole story" (p. 40). Looking at this from a population level, Kaysen suspects species may benefit from having the "majority of can-do types mixed with a significant minority of worriers and brooders" (p. 40).

Kaysen acknowledges that people who insist on drawing a bright line between clinical depression and depression more broadly will not be convinced. But she finds that for her the distinction is too blurry to be much use. If you rely on the distinction too heavily, the result is a futile "competition" about who is "more depressed" and about whether some "things in life were truly sad and worth feeling depressed about" (Kaysen 2002, 42). The distinction feeds a "pathologizing" culture that raises extraordinary hopes for a cure of ailments that "have plagued people for millennia," and it leaves people with "unreasonable expectations for happiness" (p. 41). Kaysen does not try to argue with those who find the "disease" model helpful (and she is aware that many people do), but for her depression is not a disease because it allows her to "perceive, and more important, to tolerate the fundamental ambiguities of life" (p. 45). After all, "the transient nature of happiness, beauty, success, and health may come as a shock to the upbeat person but it's old hat to the depressive" (p. 45).

Finally, Joshua Wolf Shenk gives a good sense in his memoir how an awareness of the mysteries and multiplicities of depression can be a tool of coping. Looking at the history of depression and the role of metaphor in shaping what we know about depression, Shenk suggests that:

> what we call "depression," like the mythical black bile, is a chimera . . . It is cobbled together of so many different parts, causes, experiences, and affects as to render the word ineffectual and perhaps even noxious to a full, true narrative.
>
> (Shenk 2002, 245)

Even so, the pain and suffering of depression are anything but a chimera, and Shenk understands our inevitable need to "abbreviate and simplify" in trying to understand depression (p. 246). There seems to be "no way around words like 'depression' and 'melancholy' . . . but it is one thing to use shorthand while straining against the limits of language. It is quite another to mistake such brevities for the face of suffering" (p. 246). For Shenk, simplified phrases such as "biochemical malfunctions" and "biological brain diseases" favored by well-intentioned activists and pharmaceutical companies can mystify as much as they inform:

> When we funnel a sea of human experience into the linguistic equivalent of a laboratory beaker, when we discuss suffering in simple terms of broken or fixed, mad and sane, depressed and "treated successfully," we choke the long streams of breath needed to tell of a life in whole.
>
> (Shenk 2002, 247)

This awareness allowed Shenk to consciously seek an array of different approaches to his depression. He gave medications a try (though he found none that were helpful), and he sought solace and guidance in several hundred afternoons of psychotherapy. He worked through the pain of his parents' divorce when he was seven—"the slow leakage of affection and kindness from my parents' marriage, the grim entrance of resentment, confusion, and anger" (p. 255). And he overcame his automatic tendency from his family life that "forbade expressing these emotions" (p. 255). All of this work went into the larger task of creating a story for his life that put his depression in perspective:

> to find my story by living it, following moments of emotional clarity through life's maze. I look for help in therapy, [but also] in relationships, and faith in its broadest sense—faith in the gardener, the faith of the lover, the faith of the writer. The faith that I can experience what is real about the world, that I can hurt plainly, love ravenously, feel purely, and be strong enough to go on.
>
> (Shenk 2002, 254)

Reading these depression memoirs echoes Ridge's qualitative study that many people use a range of approaches as recovery tools. Shenk is the most conscious of the process, but many other memoir writers combine approaches to depression. Lesley Dormen, for example, not only uses an unresolved grief model, she also finds creative expression and medications invaluable for coping with depression (Dormen 2002, 240). William Styron, who has the most muscular biochemical model of the group, also sees loss as a key element of his sadness (Styron 2002, 117, 125). And throughout the memoirs there are writers who combine models from cognitive, humanistic, family, and political (particularly feminist) approaches. But there are also memoir writers who are adamant about a single model approach. Liza Porter, for example, discredits the other models she previously tried once she settles on a disease model (Porter 2008, 157). And David Budbill argues strongly against a society that tries to reduce the spiritual dimensions of depression to a pathology that should be treated or a disease that should be medicated (Budbill 2008, 91).

Conclusion

The implications for clinical encounters of the multiple models for depression are many. Psychiatric practitioners would do well to develop their awareness and competency with regard to multiple models. They need to understand the many models of depression and the narrative dimensions of these models, and they must come to appreciate the many stories of biopsychiatry, psychoanalysis, cognitive therapy, family therapy, humanistic approaches, political approaches, spiritual approaches, and creative approaches, just to name a few. Furthermore, they must come to understand the value of biography, autobiography, literature, and narrative theory for developing a narrative repertoire. Clinical competency for depression means a tremendous familiarity with the many possible stories of sadness. The more stories clinicians know, the more likely they are to help their clients find a narrative frame that works for them. In addition, the more stories clinicians know, the easier it is for clinicians to appreciate that the person who should decide is the person whose life is at stake.

For sufferers of sadness, the multiple models of depression mean that there are a range of possible therapies and healing solutions that might be helpful. An approach that is right for one person may not be right for another. There must be a fit between the person and the approach, and people should feel empowered to take seriously their own intuitions and feelings. If the person getting help does not feel this fit, they are likely right. There may well be another approach, or an additional combination of approaches, that would work better with the person's proclivities. Like everything else, however, therapeutic experiences of all kinds can be frustrating, slow, and uncertain. How does one know when an approach misses their needs and when it is something that will take time, patience, and perseverance to be helpful? There can be no gold standard or simple answers to these questions. Only judgment, wisdom, and trial and error can decide.

NOTES

1. Textbooks consulted for this review include: *The American Psychiatric Publishing Textbook of Clinical Psychiatry* (Hales, Yudofsky, and Gabbard 2010); *The American Psychiatric Publishing Textbook of Mood Disorders* (Stein, Kupfer, and Schatzberg 2006); *Kaplan and Sadock's Comprehensive Textbook of Psychiatry*, 9th edition (Sadock, Sadock, and Ruiz 2009); *Handbook of Medical Psychiatry*, 2nd edition (Moore and Jefferson 2004); *Current Diagnosis and Treatment in Psychiatry* (Ebert et al. 2008); *Introductory Textbook of Psychiatry*, 4th edition (Andreason and Black 2006); *Manic-depressive Illness: Bipolar Disorder and Recurrent Depression*, 2nd edition (Goodwin and Jamison 2007); and *Textbook of Cultural Psychiatry* (Bhugra and Bhui 2007).

2. Horwitz and Wakefield use "*DSM-III*" when referring specifically to this manual. They use "*DSM*" in a more generalized way to refer to *DSM-III* and the revisions that came after it. I follow their usage for the remainder of this essay.

3. For purposes of clarity and space, this chapter will focus on aspects of these models that are particular to the model. It should be understood, however, that the deeper one gets into the model the more model adherents attempt to integrate the model with other issues and variables found in alternative models. Indeed, many strong model adherents will argue with the very idea of different models because they feel that their particular model is the only model needed to cover all issues.

4. Looking through a longer historical sweep, it would perhaps be more appropriate to refer to this period as the "second era" of biological psychiatry—with the "first era" being the Greek humoral theories discussed earlier.

5. For an extended discussion of the clinical uses of narrative, see my *Narrative Psychiatry: How Stories Can Shape the Clinical Encounter* (Lewis 2011).

6. For extensive reviews of the Dodo verdict see: Bruce Wampold, *The Great Psychotherapy Debate* (2001) and Lester Luborsky et. al., "The Dodo Bird Verdict is Alive and Well-Mostly" (2002).

REFERENCES

American Psychiatric Association. 2000. *Diagnostic and statistical manual of mental disorders*, 4th edition, text revision. Washington, DC: APA Press.

Andreason, N. 1984. *The broken brain: The biological revolution in psychiatry.* New York: Harper and Row.

Andreason, N. and Black, D. 1995. *Introductory textbook of psychiatry*, 2nd edition. Washington, DC: American Psychiatric Press.

Andreason, N. and Black, D. 2006. *Introductory textbook of psychiatry*, 4th edition. Washington, DC: American Psychiatric Press.

Angell, M. 2005. *The truth about drug companies: How they deceive us and what to do about it.* New York: Random House.

Angell, M. 2008. Industry-sponsored clinical research: A broken system. *Journal of American Medical Association.* 300: 9, 1069–1071.

Applbaum, K. 2004. *The marketing era: From professional practice to global provisioning.* New York: Routledge.

Applbaum, K. 2006. Educating for global mental health: The adoption of SSRIs in Japan. In A. Petryna, A. Lakoff, and A. Kleinman, eds. *Global pharmaceuticals: Ethics, markets, practices.* Durham, NC: Duke University Press.

Applbaum, K. 2009. Getting to yes: Corporate power and the creation of a psychopharmaceutical blockbuster. *Culture, Medicine, and Psychiatry.* 33: 2, 185–215.

Applbaum, K. 2010. Marketing global health care: The practices of big pharma. In L. Panitch and C. Leys, eds. *Morbid symptoms: Health under capitalism.* 95–115. New York: Monthly Review Press.

Aristotle. 2000. Problems connected with thought, intelligence, and wisdom. In J. Radden, ed. *The nature of melancholia: From Aristotle to Kristeva.* 57–60. Oxford: Oxford University Press.

Banks, R. 2002. An ars poetica with attitude. In N. Casey, ed. *Unholy ghost: Writers on depression.* 29–38. New York: Harper Perennial.

Barker, P. 1986. *Basic family therapy*, 2nd edition. New York: Oxford University Press.

Beck, A. and Newman, C. 2005. Cognitive therapy. In B. Sadock and V. Sadock, eds. *Kaplan and Sadock's comprehensive textbook of psychiatry*, 8th edition. 2596–2611. Philadelphia, PA: Lippincott Williams and Wilkins.

Beck, A., Rush, J., Shaw, B., and Emery, G. 1979. *Cognitive therapy of depression*. New York: Guilford Press.

Becvar, D. and Becvar, R. 2003. *Family therapy: A systemic integration*, 5th edition. Boston, MA: Allyn and Bacon.

Berlin. R. 2008. *Poets on Prozac: Mental illness, treatment and the creative process*. Baltimore, MD: Johns Hopkins University Press.

Bhugra, D. and Bhui, K. 2007. *Textbook of cultural psychiatry*. Cambridge: Cambridge University Press.

Bolton, D. 2009. Book reviews: The loss of sadness. *The British Journal of Psychiatry*. 194: 471–472.

Bracken, P. 2007. Beyond models, beyond paradigms: The radical interpretation of recovery. In P. Stasney and P. Lehmann, eds. *Alternatives beyond psychiatry*. Berlin: Peter Lehman Publishing.

Bracken, P. and Thomas, P. 2005. *Postpsychiatry: Mental health in postmodern world*. Oxford: Oxford University Press.

Breggin, P. 1994. *Talking back to Prozac: What doctors aren't telling you about today's most controversial drugs*. New York: St. Martin's Press.

Brooks, P. 1984. *Reading for the plot: Design and intention in narrative*. Cambridge, MA: Harvard University Press.

Budbill, D. 2008. The uses of depression: The way around is through. In R. Berlin, ed. *Poets on Prozac: Mental illness, treatment and the creative process*. 80–92. Baltimore, MD: Johns Hopkins University Press.

Burton, R. 1989. *The anatomy of melancholy*. Oxford: Clarendon Press.

Casey, N. 2002. *Unholy ghost: Writers on depression*. New York: Harper Perennial.

Cassian, J. 2000. Of the spirit of Accidie. In J. Radden, ed. *The nature of melancholia: From Aristotle to Kristeva*. Oxford: Oxford University Press.

Clark, H. 2008. *Narratives and depression: Telling the dark*. Albany, NY: State University of New York.

Clarke, A., Mamo, L., Fosket, J., Fishman, J., and Shim, J. eds. 2010. *Biomedicalization: Technoscience, health and illness in the U.S.* Durham, NC: Duke University Press.

Coe, J. 2000. Musings on the dark night of the soul: Insights from St. John of the Cross on developmental spirituality. *Journal of Psychology and Theology*. 28: 4, 293–307.

Comas-Diaz, L. 1994. An integrative approach. In L. Comas-Diaz and B. Green, eds. *Women of color: Integrating ethnic and gender identities in psychotherapy*. New York: The Guilford Press.

Comas-Diaz, L. 2000. An ethnopolitical approach to working with people of color. *American Psychologist*. November, 1319–1324.

Crister, G. 2005. *Generation Rx: How prescription drugs are altering American lives, minds and bodies*. New York: Houghton Mifflin Company.

Davis, L. and Morris, D. 2007. Biocultures manifesto. *New Literary History*. 38: 411–418.

Delgado, P. and Moreno, F. 2006. Neurochemistry of mood disorders. In D. Stein, D. Kupfer, and A. Schatzberg, eds. *The American Psychiatric Publishing textbook of mood disorders*. 1101–1117. Washington, DC: American Psychiatric Publishing.

Dormen, L. 2002. Planet no. In N. Casey, ed. *Unholy ghost: Writers on depression.* 229–242. New York: Harper Perennial.

Double, D. 2006. *Critical psychiatry: The limits of madness.* New York: Palgrave.

Drabkin, I. E. 1955. Remarks on ancient psychopathology. *Isis.* 46: 4, 223–234.

Duncan, B., Miller, S., Wampold, B., and Hubble, M. eds. 2009. *The heart and soul of change, second edition: Delivering what works in therapy.* Washington, DC: American Psychological Association.

Ebert, M., Loosen, P., Nurcombe, B., and Leckman, J. 2008. *Current diagnosis and treatment in psychiatry.* USA: McGraw-Hill.

Edwards, D. 2004. *Art therapy.* London: Sage Publications.

Engel, G. 1977. The need for a new medical model: A challenge to biomedicine. *Science.* 196: 4286, 129–196.

Engel, G. 1980. The clinical application of the biopsychosocial model. *American Journal of Psychiatry.* 137: 5, 535–544.

Ficino, M. 2000. Three books of life. In J. Radden, ed. *The nature of melancholia: From Aristotle to Kristeva.* Oxford: Oxford University Press.

Fisher, R. and Fisher, S., 1996. Antidepressants for children: Is scientific support necessary? *Journal of Nervous and Mental Disease.* 184: 99–102.

Foucault, M. 2006. *History of madness.* London: Routledge.

Frank, J. and Frank, J. 1991. *Persuasion and healing: A comparative study of psychotherapy.* Baltimore, MD: Johns Hopkins University Press.

Freud, S. 1959. An autobiographical study. In J. Strachey, ed. *The standard edition of the complete psychological works of Sigmund Freud,* 20: 3–71. London: Hogarth Press.

Fulford, K. W. M. 2004. Facts/Values: Ten principles of values-based medicine. In J. Radden, ed. *The philosophy of psychiatry: A companion.* Oxford: Oxford University Press.

Fulford, K. W. M, and Colombo, A. 2004. Six models of mental disorder: A study combining linguistic-analytic and empirical methods. *Philosophy, Psychiatry, & Psychology.* 11: 2, 129–144.

Fulford, K. W. M., Thornton, T., and Graham, G. 2006. *Oxford textbook of philosophy and psychiatry.* Oxford: Oxford University Press.

Gaudiano, B. and Herbert, J. 2003. Antidepressant-placebo debate in the media: Balanced coverage of placebo hype? *Scientific Review of Mental Health Practice,* 2: 1.

Gaw, A. 2010. Cultural issues. In R. Hales, S. Yudofsky, and G. Gabbard, eds. *The American Psychiatric Publishing textbook of clinical psychiatry,* 5th edition. Washington, DC: American Psychiatric Publishing.

Giere, R. 2000. The sceptical perspective: Science without the laws of nature. In J. McErlean *Philosophies of science: From foundations to contemporary issues.* 180–189. Belmont, CA: Wadsworth.

Glenmullen, J. 2000. *Prozac backlash: overcoming the dangers of Prozac, Zoloft, Paxil, and other antidepressants with safe, effective alternatives.* New York: Touchstone.

Goethe, J. W. 1971. *The sorrows of young Werther and novella.* Translated by E. Mayer and L. Bogan. New York: Vintage Books.

Goffman, E. 1961. *Asylums: Essays on the social situation of mental patients and other inmates.* New York: Doubleday.

Goldenberg, I. and Goldenberg, H. 2005. Family therapy. In R. Corsini and D. Wedding, eds. *Current Psychotherapies,* 7th edition. 372–405. Belmont, CA: Brooks/Cole-Thomson.

Goodwin, F. and Jamison, K. R. 2007. *Manic-depressive illness: Bipolar disorders and recurrent depression*, 2nd edition. Oxford: Oxford University Press.

Greenberg, R. 1999. Common psychological factors in psychiatric drug therapy. In M. Hubble, B. Duncan, and S. Miller, eds. *The heart and soul of change: What works in therapy*. Washington, DC: American Psychological Association.

Greenberg, G. 2010. *Manufacturing depression: The secret history of a modern disease*. New York: Simon and Schuster.

Greider, K. 2003. *The big fix: How the pharmaceutical industry rips off American consumers*. New York: Public Affairs.

Guest, J. 1976. *Ordinary people*. New York: Ballantine Books.

Hanisch, C. 1971. The personal is political. In J. Agel, ed. *Radical therapist: The radical therapist collection*. New York: Ballantine Books.

Hales, R., Yudofsky, S., and Gabbard, G. 2010. *The American Psychiatric Publishing textbook of clinical psychiatry*, 5th edition. Washington, DC: American Psychiatric Publishing.

Healy, D. 2004. Shaping the intimate: Influence on the experience of everyday nerves. *Social Studies of Science*. 34: 2, 219–245.

Healy, D. 2006. Manufacturing consensus. *Culture, Medicine and Psychiatry*. 30: 135–156.

Hefferman, V. 2002. A delicious placebo. In N. Casey, ed. *Unholy ghost: Writers on depression*. 8–21. New York: Harper Perennial.

Hesse, M. 2000. The explanatory function of metaphor. In J. McErlean *Philosophies of science: From foundations to contemporary issues*. 349–355. Belmont, CA: Wadsworth.

Homer. 2006. *The illiad*. Translated by Ian Johnston. Arlington, VA: Richer Resources Publishing.

Hopper, K. 2007. Rethinking social recovery in schizophrenia: What a capabilities approach might offer. *Social Science and Medicine*. 65: 5, 868–879.

Horrigan, J. 2005. To those who are bipolar, it isn't a disease—it's a gift. *Times Herald-Record*. June 5, p. 11.

Horwitz, A. and Wakefield, J. 2007. *The loss of sadness: How psychiatry transformed normal sorrow into depressive disorder*. Oxford: Oxford University Press.

Huber, C. 1999. *The depression book: Depression as an opportunity for spiritual growth*. Murphys, CA: Keep it Simple Books.

Humm, M. ed. 1992. *Modern feminisms: Political, literary, cultural*. New York: Columbia University Press.

Icarus Project. 2004. *Navigating the space between brilliance and madness: A reader of bipolar worlds*. New York: The Icarus Project.

Icarus Project. 2006. *Friends make the best medicine: A guide to creating community mental health support networks*. New York: The Icarus Project.

Jack, D. C. 1991. *Silencing the self: Women and depression*. Cambridge, MA: Harvard University Press.

Jackson, S. 1986. *Melancholia and depression: From Hippocratic times to modern times*. New Haven, CT: Yale University Press.

James, W. 1982. *The varieties of religious experience*. Harmondsworth: Penguin Classics.

Joska, J. and Stein, D. 2010. Mood disorders. In R. Hales, S. Yudofsky, and G. Gabbard, eds. *The American Psychiatric Publishing textbook of clinical psychiatry*, 5th edition. Washington, DC: American Psychiatric Publishing.

Kandel, E. 1998. A new intellectual framework for psychiatry. *American Journal of Psychiatry*. 155: 5, 457–469.

Kaysen, S. 2002. One cheer for melancholy. In N. Casey, ed. *Unholy ghost: Writers on depression*. 38–44. New York: Harper Perennial.

Kirmayer, L. 2002. Psychopharmacology in a globalizing world: The use of antidepressants in Japan. *Transcultural Psychiatry*. 39: 3, 295–322.

Kirmayer, L. 2004. The cultural diversity of healing: Meaning, metaphor and mechanism. *British Medical Bulletin*. 69: 33–48.

Kirmayer, L. and Jarvis, E. 2006. Depression across cultures. In D. Stein, D. Kupfer, and A. Schatzberg, eds. *The American Psychiatric Publishing textbook of mood disorders*. 699–717. Washington, DC: American Psychiatric Publishing.

Kirsch, I. and Sapirstein, G. 1998. Listening to Prozac but hearing placebo: A meta-analysis of antidepressant medications. *Prevention and Treatment*. 1, 2a. Available at: http://journals.apa.org/prevention/volume1.

Kirsch, I., Moore, T. J., Scoboria, A., and Nicholls, S. 2002. The emperor's new drugs: An analysis of antidepressant medication data submitted to the U.S. Food and Drug Administration. *Prevention and Treatment*, 5, 23. Available at: http://journals.apa.org/prevention/volume5.

Klein, D. 1998. Listening to meta-analysis but hearing bias. *Prevention and treatment*. 1, 6c. Available at: http://journals.apa.org/prevention/volume1.

Kleinman, A. 1977. Depression, somatization and the new cross-cultural psychiatry. *Social Science and Medicine*. 11: 3–10.

Kleinman, A. 1988. *Rethinking psychiatry: From cultural category to personal experience*. New York: Free Press.

Kleinman, A. 2004. Culture and depression. *New England Journal of Medicine*. 351: 951–953.

Kleinman, A. and Good, B. 1985. Meanings, relationships, social affects: Historical and anthropological perspectives on depression. In A. Kleinman and B. Good, eds. *Culture and depression: Studies in anthropology and cross-cultural psychiatry of affect and disorder*. 1–43. Berkley, CA: University of California Press.

Kraepelin, E. 2000. Manic-depressive insanity. In J. Radden, ed. *The nature of melancholia: From Aristotle to Kristeva*. 260–279. Oxford: Oxford University Press.

Kramer, P. 2005. *Against depression*. New York: Viking.

Laing, R. D. 1967. *The politics of experience*. New York: Pantheon Books.

Laing, R. D. 1968. The obvious. In D. Cooper, ed. *The dialectics of liberation*. Harmondsworth: Penguin.

Lakoff, G. and Johnson, M. 1980. *Metaphors we live by*. Chicago, IL: University of Chicago Press.

Lewis, B. 2006a. *Moving beyond Prozac, DSM, and the new psychiatry: The birth of postpsychiatry*. Ann Arbor, MI: University of Michigan Press.

Lewis, B. 2006b. A mad fight: Psychiatry and disability activism. In L. Davis, ed. *Disability studies reader*, 2nd edition. New York: Routledge.

Lewis, B. 2007. High theory/mass markets: Newsweek magazine and the circuits of medical culture. *Perspectives in Biology and Medicine*. 50: 3, 363–378.

Lewis, B. 2011. *Narrative psychiatry: How stories can shape clinical practice*. Baltimore, MD: Johns Hopkins University Press.

Lock, M. 1993. *Encounters with aging: Mythologies of menopause in Japan and North America*. Berkeley, CA: University of California Press.

Luborsky, L., Rosenthal, R., Diguer, L., Andrusyna, T., Berman, J. S., Levitt, J. T., Seligman, D. and Krause, E. 2002. The dodo bird verdict is alive and well—Mostly. *Clinical psychology: Science and Practice*, 9: 1, 2–12.

Martin, E. 2007. *Biopolar expeditions: Mania and depression in American culture*. Princeton, NJ: Princeton University Press.

Martin, P. 1999. *The Zen path through depression*. San Francisco: HarperSan-Francisco.

Matheson, A. 2008. Corporate science and the husbandry of scientific and medical knowledge by the pharmaceutical industry. *BioSocieties*. 3: 355–382.

Mills, M. (director). 2007. *Does your soul have a cold?* New York: Rainbow Media.

Mirowsky, J. and Ross, C. 2003. *Social causes of psychological distress*. New York: Aldine de Gruyter.

Mitchell, S. 2004. *Gilgamesh: A new English version*. New York: Free Press.

Moncrieff, J. 2009. *The myth of the chemical cure: A critique of psychiatric drug treatment*. London: Palgrave Macmillan.

Moore, D. and Jefferson, J. W. 2004. *Handbook of medical psychiatry*, 2nd edition. Philadelphia, PA: Mosby.

Moore, T. 2004. *Dark nights of the soul: A guide for finding your way through life's ordeals*. New York: Gotham Books.

Morrison, L. 2005. *Talking back to psychiatry: The consumer/survivor/ex-patient movement*. New York: Routledge.

Moynihan, R., Heath, I., and Henry, D. 2002. Selling sickness: the pharmaceutical industry and disease mongering. *British Medical Journal*. 324: 886–891.

Narrow, W. and Rubio-Stipec, M. 2009. Epidemiology. In B. Sadock, V. Sadock, and P. Ruiz, eds. *Kaplan and Sadock's comprehensive textbook of psychiatry*, 9th edition. 754–771. Philadelphia, PA: Lippincott Williams and Wilkins.

Nobler, M. and Sackeim, A. 2006. Electroconvulsive therapy and transcranial magnetic stimulation. In D. Stein, D. Kupfer, and A. Schatzberg, eds. *The American Psychiatric Publishing textbook of mood disorders*. 317–337. Washington, DC: American Psychiatric Publishing.

Norris, K. 2008. *Acedia and me: A marriage, monks, and a writer's life*. New York: Riverhead Books.

Obeyesekere, G. 1985. Depression, Buddhism, and the work of culture in Sri Lanka. In A. Kleinman and B. Good, eds. *Culture and depression: Studies in anthropology and cross-cultural psychiatry of affect and disorder*. 1–43. Berkeley, CA: University of California Press.

Oldani, M. 2004. Thick prescriptions: Toward an interpretation of pharmaceutical sales practices. *Medical anthropological quarterly*. 18: 3, 325–326.

Petersen, M. 2000. What's black and white and sells medicine? *New York Times*, August 27.

Petryna, A., Lakoff, A., and Kleinman, A. eds. 2006. *Global pharmaceuticals: Ethics, markets, practices*. Durham, NC: Duke University Press.

Pollock, G. 1978. Process and affect: Mourning and grief. *International Journal of Psychoanalysis*. 59: 255–276.

Pollock, G. 1989. *The mourning-liberation process*. Madison, CT: International Universities Press.

Porter, L. 2008. Down the tracks Bruce Springsteen sang to me. In R. Berlin, ed. *Poets on Prozac: Mental illness, treatment and the creative process*. 147–161. Baltimore, MD: Johns Hopkins University Press.

Porter, R. 2002. *Madness: A brief history*. Oxford: Oxford University Press.

Potter, W., Padich, R., Rudorfer, M., and Krishnan, R. 2006. Tricylics, tetracyclics, and monoamine oxidase inhibitors. In D. Stein, D. Kupfer, and A. Schatzberg, eds. *The American Psychiatric Publishing textbook of mood disorders*. 251–263. Washington, DC: American Psychiatric Publishing.

Quitkin, F., Rabkin, J. G., Gerald, J., Davis, J. M., and Klein, D. F. 2000. Validity of clinical trials of antidepressants. *American Journal of Psychiatry*. 157: 327–337.

Radden, J. 2000. *The nature of melancholia: From Aristotle to Kristeva*. Oxford: Oxford University Press.

Rajkowska, G. 2006. Anatomical Pathology, In D. Stein, D. Kupfer, and A. Schatzberg, eds. *The American Psychiatric Publishing textbook of mood disorders*. 179–197. Washington, DC: American Psychiatric Publishing.

Rampton, S. and Stauber, J. 2001. *Trust us, we're experts! How industry manipulates science and gambles with your future*. New York: Tarcher/Putnam.

Raskin, N. and Rogers, C. 2005. Person-centered therapy. In R. Corsini and D. Wedding, eds. *Current psychotherapies*, 7th edition. 238–269. Belmont, CA: Brooks/Cole-Thomson.

Rice, L. and Greenberg, L. 1992. Humanistic approaches to psychology. In D. Freedheim, ed. *History of psychotherapy: A century of change*. 197–225. Washington, DC: American Psychological Association.

Ricoeur, P. 1984. *Time and narrative*. Vol 1. Chicago, IL: University of Chicago Press.

Ricoeur, P. 1991. Life in quest of narrative. In D. Wood, ed. *On Paul Ricoeur: Narrative and interpretation*. London: Routledge.

Ricoeur, P. 1992. *Oneself as another*. Chicago, IL: University of Chicago Press.

Ridge, D. 2009. *Recovery from depression using the narrative approach: A guide for doctors, complementary therapist, and mental health professionals*. London: Jessica Kingsley Publishers.

Ridge, D. and Zeibland, S. 2006. "The old me could never have done that": How people give meaning to recovery following depression. *Qualitative Healthcare Research*. 16: 8, 1038–1053.

Rihmer, Z. and Angst, J. 2009. Mood disorders: Epidemiology. In B. Sadock, V. Sadock, and P. Ruiz, eds. *Kaplan and Sadock's comprehensive textbook of psychiatry*, 9th edition. 1645–1653. Philadelphia, PA: Lippincott Williams and Wilkins.

Rogers, C. 1961. *On becoming a person*. Boston, MA: Houghton Mifflin Company.

Rose, N. 2003. Neurochemical selves. *Society*. Nov/Dec: 46–59.

Rose, N. 2006. Disorders without borders? The expanding scope of psychiatric practice. *BioSocieties*. 1: 465–484.

Rosenzweig, S. 1936. Some implicit common factors in diverse methods of psychotherapy: At last the Dodo said, "Everybody has won and all must have prizes." *American Journal of Orthopsychiatry*. 6: 412–415.

Sadock, B., Sadock, V., and Ruiz, P. 2009. *Kaplan and Sadock's comprehensive textbook of psychiatry*, 9th edition. Philadelphia, PA: Lippincott Williams and Wilkins.

Saito, S., Mukoharaz, K., and Bito, S. 2010. Japanese practicing physicians' relationship with pharmaceutical representatives: A national survey. *Plos One*. 5: 8, e 12193.

Saxe, J. G. 1873. *The poems of John Godfrey Saxe: Complete edition*. Boston, MA: James R. Osgood and Company.

Scheff, T. *Being mentally ill: A sociological theory*. Chicago, IL: Aldine Press.

Schreurs, A. 2002. *Psychotherapy and spirituality: Integrating the spiritual dimension into therapeutic practice.* London: Jessica Kingsley Publishers.

Schulz, K. 2004. Did antidepressants depress Japan? *New York Times*, August 22.

Schwary, R. (producer) and Redford, R. (director). 1980. *Ordinary people* [Motion picture]. Hollywood, CA: Paramount Pictures.

Shaffer, J. 1978. *Humanistic psychology.* Upper Saddle River, NJ: Prentice Hall.

Shelton, R. and Lester, N. 2006. Selective serotonin reuptake inhibitor and newer antidepressants. In D. Stein, D. Kupfer, and A. Schatzberg, eds. *The American Psychiatric Publishing textbook of mood disorders.* 263–281. Washington, DC: American Psychiatric Publishing.

Shenk, J. W. 2002. A melancholy of my own. In N. Casey, ed. *Unholy ghost: Writers on depression.* 242–256. New York: Harper Perennial.

Shorter, E. 1997. *A history of psychiatry: From the era of the asylum to the age of Prozac.* New York: John Wiley and Sons.

Simon, B. 1978. *Mind and madness in ancient Greece: The classical roots of modern psychiatry.* Ithaca, NY: Cornel University Press.

Singh, J., Quiroz, J., Gould, T., Zarate, C., and Manji, H. 2006. Molecular and Cellular Neurobiology of severe mood disorders. In D. Stein, D. Kupfer, and A. Schatzberg, eds. *The American Psychiatric Publishing textbook of mood disorders.* 197–219. Washington, DC: American Psychiatric Publishing.

Sismondo, S. 2007. Ghost management: How much of the medical literature is shaped behind the scenes by the pharmaceutical industry? *PLOS Medicine.* 4: 9, 1429–1433.

Sismondo, S. 2008. How pharmaceutical industry funding affects trial outcomes: Causal structures and responses. *Social Science and Medicine.* 66: 1909–1914.

Smith, R. 2005. Medical journals are an extension of the marketing arm of pharmaceutical companies. *PLoS Medicine 2,* 5:364–366.

Solomon, A. 2001. *The noonday demon: An atlas of depression.* New York: Scribner.

Sophocles. 1999. *Aiax* [Ajax]. H. Golder and R. Pevear translators. Oxford: Oxford University Press.

Sparks, J., Duncan, B., Cohen, D., and Antonuccio, D. 2009. Psychiatric drugs and common factors: An evaluation of risks and benefits for clinical practice. In B. Duncan, S. Miller, B. Wampold, and M. Hubble, eds. *The heart and soul of change, second edition: delivering what works in therapy.* Washington, DC: American Psychological Association.

Stein, D. J., Kupfer, D. J. and Schatzberg, A. F. 2006. *The American Psychiatric Publishing textbook of mood disorders.* Washington, DC: American Psychiatric Publishing.

Sowers, W. and Thompson, K. eds. 2007. *Keystones for collaboration and leadership: Issues and recommendations for the transformation of community psychiatry.* Available at www.communitypsychiatry.org/aacp/TransformationofPsychiatryReport.pdf.

Styron, W. 2002. *From Darkness visible.* In N. Casey, ed. *Unholy ghost: Writers on depression.* 114–126. New York: Harper Perennial.

Szasz, T. 1961. *The myth of mental illness: Foundations of a theory of personal conduct.* New York: Hoeber-Harper.

Tamini, S. and Cohen, C. eds. 2008 *Liberatory psychiatry.* Cambridge: Cambridge University Press.

Taylor, C. 2002. *Varieties of religion today.* Cambridge, MA: Harvard University Press.

Twichell, C. 2002. An ars poetica under the influence. In N. Casey, ed. *Unholy ghost: Writers on depression.* 21–29. New York: Harper Perennial.

Tyrer, P. and Steinberg, P. 2005. *Models for mental disorder*, 4th edition. Chichester: John Wiley and Sons.

Vedantam, S. (2002, May 7). Against depression, a sugar pill is hard to beat. *Washington Post*, A01. Available at: www.washingtonpost.com/ac2/wp-dyn/A42930-2002May6.

Vickery, K. 2010. Widening the psychiatric gaze: Reflections on *Psychodoctor*, depression, and recent transitions in Japanese mental health care. *Transcultural Psychiatry*. 47: 3, 363–391.

Wampold, B. E. 2001. *The great psychotherapy debate*. Mahwah, NJ: Lawrence Erlbaum Associates.

Weintraub, A. 2004. *Yoga for depression*. New York: Broadway Books.

WHO World Mental Health Survey Consortium. 2004. Prevalence, severity, and unmet need for treatment of mental disorders in the World Health Organization world mental health surveys. *Journal of the American Medical Association*. 291: 21, 2581–2590.

Williams, D. and Neighbors, H. 2006. Social perspectives on mood disorders. In D. Stein, D. Kupfer, and A. Schatzberg, eds. *The American Psychiatric Publishing textbook of mood disorders*. 145–159. Washington, DC: American Psychiatric Publishing.

Wilson, D. 2008. *Against happiness: In praise of melancholy*. New York: Sarah Crichton Books.

Index